An Introduction to Risk and Return from Common Stocks   *Richard A. Brealey*

The M.I.T. Press
Massachusetts Institute of Technology
Cambridge, Massachusetts, and London, England

Second Printing, October 1970

ISBN 0 262 02047 5 (hardcover)

Library of Congress catalog card number: 69–12751

Preface

Buoyant stock markets, a growing interest in the theory of financial management, and the availability of computers have all contributed to inspire the production in the last ten years of a large number of statistical studies related to common stock investment. Because work in this field is usually addressed to statisticians and either appears in academic journals or goes unpublished, much of it escapes the attention of the person to whom it could be of most use, namely, the investor.

This book is intended primarily for the professional investor or the finance student. It assumes no prior knowledge of statistics and does not, for the most part, seek to impart such knowledge.

It aims to provide in three largely self-contained sections a description of the stock market as seen through the eyes of the statistician. Since the reader is unlikely to be convinced by bald statements of conclusions, the evidence on any topic is outlined, together with an assessment of its reliability. This is followed by suggested explanations and a brief comment on the implications. The tone of the book, therefore, is descriptive, not prescriptive. It offers no philosopher's stone nor road to easy riches, but it is hoped that by adding to the reader's knowledge of the environment in which he is operating and by questioning certain items of dogma, it may assist him to become a better investor. It is only hoped that the reader, in the process of learning something of the theory of investment, does not suffer the fate of the unfortunate centipede.

The centipede was happy, quite
Until the toad in fun
Said "Pray which leg goes after which?"
Which drove her mind to such a pitch
She lay distracted in a ditch
Considering how to run.

Such a publication is not likely to prove easy reading under any circumstances. There is an obligation, therefore, to keep it short. In consequence, this book is neither comprehensive nor exhaustive. The criteria for selection of a topic are that it is fundamental and that quantitative evidence is available.

R. A. B.

June 1968
Cambridge, Mass.

Acknowledgments

I am grateful to Professor Paul Cootner for the encouragement to write this book and for his comments on the manuscript. Other valuable suggestions for improvement came from Professor Robert Glauber and from Messrs. Ian Soutar and Tony Hampson.

My company, Keystone Custodian Funds, Inc., also offered me help and encouragement in the venture.

I should like to thank Professor Peter Williamson and the Dartmouth College Computation Center for the use of their portfolio selection program.

Margaret Lague, Peggy Schmidt, and my wife shared the labor of typing several drafts of the manuscript.

Contents

Part I: Stock Prices

based on all existing information together with all that it is believed to imply. If a fresh piece of information that affects the article's value subsequently becomes available, it and its implications will be examined and will cause a new equilibrium price to be established. This price will, in its turn, endure until a new piece of information causes it to change. Because information is only new when it has not been deduced from earlier information, its effect on prices will be quite independent of anything that may have happened earlier. This point requires emphasis. One item of news must, by definition, be independent of an earlier item of news; otherwise, it is not news. Thus, it would be quite possible for each successive price change to be independent of the preceding change and yet for the events to which these changes are indirectly related to describe quite regular progressions.

Suppose, however, that a limited group of companies or individuals begin to gain access to the same information one day in advance of the rest of the market. This could occur if they learn today of facts that the rest of the market does not learn until tomorrow and derive the same amount of information from them. Alternatively, though they do not learn of events any earlier than the rest of the market, their superior insight might allow them to derive more information from the events. In either case, the effect is the same. If the information is going to justify, in the view of the rest of the market, a rise in price, the knowledgeable individuals could secure a profit by buying the article today and selling it tomorrow. In fact, they would maximize their profits if they continued to buy in advance of their less-informed brethren until either their resources were exhausted or their actions had caused such a change in the article's price that no further profit remained. As long as the price was shifted only part way towards tomorrow's equilibrium, successive price changes would not be independent, for the price rise caused by the experts' purchases would be followed by a price rise caused by the purchases of the uninitiated. Thus, price changes will be independent of each other only when information is immediately and fully reflected in the article's price, and they will be dependent when prices reflect a spreading awareness of information.

In a perfectly free market, however, this latter situation cannot endure. At least two things will happen. First, the uninitiated will pay the experts to do their purchasing for them. Second, the uninitiated will learn to spot what the experts are doing by examining past price changes and imitating the experts' behavior. But if sufficient buyers gain the advantage of the experts, there are no uninitiated left, and the original situation is re-established. Each price change again becomes wholly independent of the price changes that preceded it.

Such would be the mechanism of price adjustment in a perfectly free and competitive market.[45] As a description of the mechanism of price determination for most goods, it is completely inadequate. As a picture of the stock market, however, it has more plausibility.

In the first place, the price of a stock is never merely an incidental consideration in the transaction, since the investor's primary motive for purchasing a stock is the belief that he will subsequently be able to sell it at a higher price. This expectation is strengthened by the knowledge that a marketplace exists, that his marketing costs do not differ substantially from those of other investors, and that these costs do not constitute a large proportion of a stock's value. This ease of entry into the market and the low cost of dealing ensure that the price is quite free to adjust to minor changes in expectations and operate as the equilibrating mechanism between supply and demand.

Not only is the stock market an extremely free market, but it appears to be a very competitive one with efficient methods of information distribution. Legal restrictions combine with moral obligations to make public companies reluctant to divulge to one group of investors what they deny to another. In this they are aided by a large brokerage community and financial press competing to retrieve, interpret, and disseminate this news. Modern media of communication also reduce the opportunities for temporary advantages.

There is no doubt that experience and effort can uncover better information for evaluating a stock. However, the effects on price behavior are limited by three considerations. As in the hypothetical ideal market, the inexperienced and part-time investor has tended increasingly to pay the full-time investor, such as the bank, mutual fund, or investment counselor, to manage his investments for him, with the result that 43% of the public business on the New York Stock Exchange (hereafter, NYSE) is now conducted by institutions.[58] Not only does this tend to make the market a market of experts, but a further leveling effect results from the difficulties, with a large portfolio, of taking advantage of any special information without immediately moving the price to its future equilibrium level. Finally, there exists a large body of "technicians" who seek to become secondhand experts by looking for any dependence in successive price changes and acting on the basis of it. By so doing, they also serve to limit this dependence.

The reader may feel that, regardless of the plausibility of this description of the process of stock price determination, the conclusion is clearly in contradiction with the obvious facts of the case. A glance at any chart of stock prices will almost always suggest clear patterns that are inconsistent with the notion of each change being independent of earlier changes. It is possible, however, that these visual impressions of price behavior are distorted by several forms of optical illusion.

Random series can often trace out perfect, or only slightly imperfect, short-term patterns. The observer who is seeking for order in an unordered environment will tend to notice these apparent regularities and ignore the exceptions. Thus, the roulette player will read meaning into even the shortest runs of good or ill fortune. As an illustration of this, the reader is invited to toss a coin twenty or so times and note the long, *almost uninterrupted* runs of heads or tails that can occur.

A more subtle form of illusion may arise from the fact that, whereas investors are uniformly interested in price changes from any level, charts of stock prices almost invariably depict the levels themselves.[43] It would be surprising if tomorrow's stock price were not usually closer to today's price than to that of a year ago, but this is a trivial piece of information and valueless for making money. Consider the following series of graphs. Figure 1 depicts the level of the Dow-Jones Average

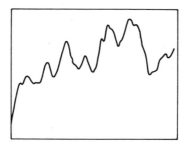

FIGURE 1. Dow-Jones Index, 1967 (after Roberts[43]).

during 1967. It appears to be characterized by typical short-term cyclical patterns. Yet, when it is reconstructed in Figure 2 as a chart of the weekly changes in the index, the symmetry disappears and is replaced by a meaningless jumble. Figures 3

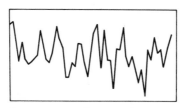

FIGURE 2. Weekly changes, Dow-Jones Index, 1967 (after Roberts[43]).

and 4 reverse the process. A set of random-number tables was used to simulate the jumbled series of price changes in Figure 3. When this, in turn, is reconstructed in Figure 4 as a chart

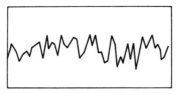

FIGURE 3. Simulated Dow-Jones changes.[43]

of the levels of these counterfeit prices, the resulting graph acquires many of the characteristics of actual charts of the market, even to the "head and shoulders" movement.

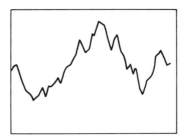

FIGURE 4. Simulated Dow-Jones Index.[43]

This does not, of course, constitute satisfactory evidence that stock prices do move randomly, but the similarity between these simulated and actual markets does justify proceeding with the next step.

A common exhibit at many museums of science is a device whereby balls are allowed to fall subject to a random amount of deflection into a number of compartments. The balls tend to cluster in the central compartment with a diminishing number in each adjacent compartment, so that they form the familiar bell-shaped pattern of a normal distribution. The model is employed to illustrate the general truth that the sum of a number of separate random events tends to be normally distributed.

The proportionate change in the price of a stock over a day, a month, or a year may be regarded as the sum of the proportionate changes over a shorter time interval. If the latter constitute a random series, the sum of these changes should, like the balls in the museum, tend to be normally distributed. To test this possibility, the 30 Dow-Jones stocks were examined for a period that differed from stock to stock but was in no case less than four and a half years, always ending in September 1962.[14] The daily proportionate price changes were computed for each stock. The number of occasions on which a change of any given magnitude occurred was then plotted on a graph. Figure 5 shows the results for six of the stocks and, for comparison, a plot of the normal distribution. In each case, the distribution of stock price changes is very similar to the normal pattern. Some of the differences between the two distributions may also be compatible with random price changes, but for the present this may be regarded as a point of detail.

It should be noted, however, that though the sums of random events will tend to form a certain pattern, the reverse is not necessarily true, so that the existence of such a pattern does not constitute proof of randomness. The balls in the museum exhibit could, for example, be arranged in their compartments by the curator. However, the normality of a distribution constitutes prima facie evidence of the randomness of the generating process.

It is never possible, in fact, to prove that a series is random. The most that can be done is to demonstrate that this or that pattern does not exist. One such demonstration may be illustrated with the aid of Figure 6. The horizontal axis represents the proportionate change in the price of a hypothetical stock over period t. The vertical axis represents the change in the

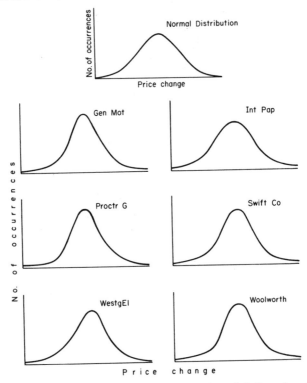

FIGURE 5. Normal distribution and distribution of daily price changes of six stocks (after Fama[14]).

stock's price over the succeeding period, $t + 1$. Each cross depicts the stock's behavior over a single time period. If the crosses are distributed incoherently over the chart, as is the case in Figure 6, it may be concluded that there is no tendency for a price change to be succeeded by a similar change. However, if the crosses group along a straight line, some regularity in price behavior is present.

It is not necessary, in practice, to draw such a graph, since its characteristics may be measured more precisely by the coefficient of correlation. This measures the extent to which the points in such a scatter diagram tend to lie along a straight line. In other words, it is simply an index of the closeness of the relationship between two sets of numbers. The correlation coefficient may take any value on a scale between minus one and

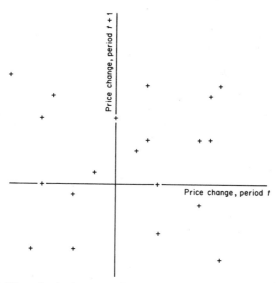

FIGURE 6. Hypothetical scatter diagram of price changes of a stock in period t and in period $t + 1$, for different values of t.

plus one. If there is no relationship, so that the crosses are scattered randomly across the graph, the coefficient will have a value of zero. A positive correlation coefficient would indicate a tendency for a high value for one series to be paralleled by a high value for the second series. In the present problem, a positive coefficient would suggest that an above-average price rise in period t tends to be paralleled by an above-average rise in the period $t + 1$. Finally, a correlation coefficient that is less than zero would indicate an inverse relationship. In the present instance, it would indicate that an above-average price rise tends to be followed by a below-average rise.

The daily proportionate price changes of the 30 Dow-Jones stocks for the approximately five years ending in 1962 were submitted to this test.[14] The resulting coefficients of correlation between the successive price changes of each stock are shown in the first column of Table 1. In no case does the coefficient differ substantially from zero, and in one-third of the instances it is negative. It is always possible for successive price changes to be unrelated but for lagged changes to exhibit some dependence. The results of comparing each day's price change with the change two days later are therefore shown in the second column of Table 1. Column 3 represents a lag of three days, and so on. On each occasion, the coefficients of correlation suggest a negligible degree of relationship.

The exercise was repeated to cover adjacent four-day, nine-day, and sixteen-day changes. The average correlation coefficients were −0.04, −0.05, and +0.01, respectively. A further study of the monthly changes of 63 selected stocks between 1927 and 1960 produced broadly similar results with an average coefficient of +0.02.[25] Yet another study that examined the weekly changes of 29 randomly chosen stocks for the period January 1951 to December 1958 produced an average coefficient of correlation for adjacent periods of −0.06.[36]

An interesting side result of this last work was that a market index, formed by averaging the changes of 25 of these stocks, did appear to exhibit a faint pattern over time, for the coefficient of correlation between adjacent weekly changes was +0.15. One might be inclined simply to attribute this result to chance, were it not supported by the fact that the coefficient of correlation between adjacent daily changes of the Dow-Jones Average from 1952 to 1963 was +0.11.[17] One effect of averaging the price changes of different stocks is to wash out the individualistic portions of the price changes, leaving only the movement that is common to all stocks. It is quite possible for this market portion of a stock's movement to exhibit depend-

TABLE 1. *Correlation coefficients between daily price changes and lagged price changes for each of the Dow-Jones stocks.*

Stocks	Lag in Days									
	1	2	3	4	5	6	7	8	9	10
AlliedCh	.02	−.04	.01	−.00	.03	.00	−.02	−.03	−.02	−.01
Alcoa	.12	.04	−.01	.02	−.02	.01	.02	.01	−.00	−.03
Am Can	−.09	−.02	.03	−.07	−.02	−.01	.02	.03	−.05	−.04
Am T&T	−.04	−.10	.00	.03	.01	−.01	.00	.03	−.01	.01
Am Tob	.11	−.11	−.06	−.07	.01	−.01	.01	.05	.04	.04
Anacond	.07	−.06	−.05	−.00	.00	−.04	.01	.02	−.01	−.06
Beth Stl	.01	−.07	.01	.02	−.05	−.10	−.01	.00	−.00	−.02
Chrysler	.01	−.07	−.02	−.01	−.02	.01	.04	.06	−.04	.02
duPont	.01	−.03	.06	.03	−.00	−.05	.02	.01	−.03	.00
E Kodak	.03	.01	−.03	.01	−.02	.01	.01	.01	.01	.00
Gen Elec	.01	−.04	−.02	.03	−.00	.00	−.01	.01	−.00	.01
Gen Fds	.06	−.00	.05	.00	−.02	−.05	−.01	−.01	−.02	−.02
GenMot	−.00	−.06	−.04	−.01	−.04	−.01	.02	.01	−.02	.01
Goodyr	−.12	.02	−.04	.04	−.00	−.00	.04	.01	−.02	.01
Int Harv	−.02	−.03	−.03	.04	−.05	−.02	−.00	.00	−.05	−.02
Int Nick	.10	−.03	−.02	.02	.03	.06	−.04	−.01	−.02	.03
Int Pap	.05	−.01	−.06	.05	.05	−.00	−.03	−.02	−.00	−.02
JohnMan	.01	−.04	−.03	−.02	−.03	−.08	.04	.02	−.04	.03
OwensIll	−.02	−.08	−.05	.07	.09	−.04	.01	−.04	.07	−.04
Proctr G	.10	−.01	−.01	.01	−.02	.02	.01	−.01	−.02	−.02
Sears Ro	.10	.03	.03	.03	.01	−.05	−.01	−.01	−.01	−.01
StOilCal	.03	−.03	−.05	−.03	−.05	−.03	−.01	.07	−.05	−.04
StOilNJ	.01	−.12	.02	.01	−.05	−.02	−.02	−.03	−.07	.08
Swift Co	−.00	−.02	−.01	.01	.06	.01	−.04	.01	.01	.00
Texaco	.09	−.05	−.02	−.02	−.02	−.01	.03	.03	−.01	.01
Un Carbide	.11	−.01	.04	.05	−.04	−.03	.00	−.01	−.05	−.04
UnitAirc	.01	−.03	−.02	−.05	−.07	−.05	.05	.04	.02	−.02
US Steel	.04	−.07	.01	.01	−.01	−.02	.04	.04	−.02	−.04
WestgEl	−.03	−.02	−.04	−.00	.00	−.05	−.02	.01	−.01	.01
Woolworth	.03	−.02	.02	.01	.01	−.04	−.01	.00	−.09	−.01
Averages	.03	−.04	−.01	.01	−.01	−.02	.00	.01	−.02	−.01

Source: After Fama.[14]

ence even though that of the stock price as a whole does not. Alternatively, these higher values for the correlation coefficient could be a statistical oddity caused by the fact that these indices are formed by averaging the prices of transactions that may not have occurred simultaneously at the market close.[55]

This same statistical approach was also used to examine weekly changes of 15 British common stock indices between 1928 and 1938.[24] The average correlation coefficient for adjacent weeks was +0.11, for lagged weeks, +0.07. In view of the comments in the last paragraph and the fact that the degree of correlation increased when even broader indices were examined, it seems quite possible that even these low figures exaggerate the amount of dependence that would have existed for individual shares.

These and similar studies raise some intriguing puzzles. For example, it is far from clear why daily and monthly price changes should be positively related and weekly changes inversely related. One conclusion, however, is apparent — in all instances the relationships are very tenuous.

Correlation coefficients, however, can sometimes be dominated by a limited number of very major exceptions to a general rule. It may be that a tendency towards a coherent pattern of price changes is being obscured by one or two instances in which a very large price rise is succeeded by a correspondingly severe fall. An alternative test that gives equal weight to each price change would therefore be useful. For this, the Dow-Jones stocks were again examined.[14] Each daily price change was simply classified as positive, zero, or negative, regardless of its magnitude, and the number of runs of successive changes of the same sign was counted. Thus the series +++−0− would be considered to comprise four runs. If there is a tendency for a move in one direction to be succeeded by a further such move, the average length of run will be longer and the total number of runs will be less than if the moves were distributed randomly.

The first column of figures in Table 2 shows the actual number of continuous runs for each Dow-Jones stock. The second column shows the number of continuous runs that could be

TABLE 2. *Total actual and expected number of runs of consecutive price changes in the same direction for each of the Dow-Jones stocks.*

Stock	Daily Changes		Four-Day Changes		Nine-Day Changes		Sixteen-Day Changes	
	Actual	Expected	Actual	Expected	Actual	Expected	Actual	Expected
AlliedCh	683	713	160	162	71	71	39	39
Alcoa	601	671	151	154	61	67	41	39
Am Can	730	756	169	172	71	73	48	44
Am T&T	657	688	165	156	66	70	34	37
Am Tob	700	747	178	173	69	73	41	41
Anacond	635	680	166	160	68	66	36	38
Beth Stl	709	720	163	159	80	72	41	42
Chrysler	927	932	223	222	100	97	54	54
duPont	672	695	160	162	78	72	43	39
E Kodak	678	679	154	160	70	70	43	40
Gen Elec	918	956	225	225	101	97	51	52
Gen Fds	799	825	185	191	81	76	43	41
GenMot	832	868	202	205	83	86	44	47
Goodyr	681	672	151	158	60	65	36	36
Int Harv	720	713	159	164	84	73	40	38
Int Nick	704	713	163	164	68	71	34	38
Int Pap	762	826	190	194	80	83	51	47
JohnMan	685	699	173	160	64	69	39	40
OwensIll	713	743	171	169	69	73	36	39
Proctr G	826	859	180	191	66	81	40	43
Sears Ro	700	748	167	173	66	71	40	35
StOilCal	972	979	237	228	97	99	59	54
StOilNJ	688	704	159	159	69	69	29	37
Swift Co	878	878	209	197	85	84	50	48
Texaco	600	654	143	155	57	63	29	36
Un Carbide	595	621	142	151	67	67	36	35
UnitAirc	661	699	172	161	77	68	45	40
US Steel	651	662	162	158	65	70	37	41
WestgEl	829	826	198	193	87	84	41	46
Woolworth	847	868	193	199	78	81	48	48
Averages	735	760	176	176	75	75	42	42

Source: After Fama.[14]

expected if the plus days and minus days were mixed in a wholly random fashion. These figures suggest a very slight tendency for runs to persist, which fits with the results of the correlation analysis of adjacent one-day changes. However, this divergence from a random series is negligible for most purposes. Indeed, when the exercise is repeated for four-, nine- and sixteen-day price changes, the distinction almost disappears.

This test was extended to consider not only the total number of runs but also the number of runs of any given duration. Again the differences between the actual and random cases proved to be very small. A similar test based on the monthly changes in a market index between 1897 and 1959 confirmed these results.[1]

The correlation technique employed earlier served to describe the relationship between each day's price change and that of a subsequent day. A more complete description of the extent of temporal dependence can be provided with the aid of spectral analysis, a technique for measuring the proportion of the variation that may be accounted for by cycles of varying lengths. Among the many series that have been analyzed with the aid of spectral analysis are the monthly changes of the Standard and Poor's Index between 1875 and 1952, the monthly changes of six common stocks between 1946 and 1960, and the weekly changes of the British Financial Times Index between 1959 and 1962.[20,21] Some of these tests found very faint evidence of a seasonal effect and of a monthly cycle. There were also traces of a 40-month cycle that might be related to the business cycle. However, in no case was a major departure from the random walk model apparent.

All these studies have suggested some possible differences between the actual behavior of stock prices and the random walk of the hypothetical perfect market. Only a limited number of the many possible relationships have been examined, so other differences from the random model may exist. Nevertheless, the most striking characteristic of the results is not so much the differences as the very close resemblance between the two series.

This chapter has examined price changes over periods varying from one day to one month; the tests have extended back to 1875 and forward to 1962; they have covered both American and British data. In no case was the random walk approximation seriously offended. The future must remain a subject for individual judgment. It is arguable that increasing concentration of funds in a few hands could diminish the degree of competition. More probably, however, improved methods of communication, the increasing professionalism of the market, and better facilities for detecting market imperfections will all contribute toward maintaining the similarity between the two series.

Before continuing in the next chapter to concentrate attention on the differences between the two markets, it might be well to pause here and take stock of some of the implications of the resemblance.

The term *random* has certain unfortunate connotations. Random events are often believed to be in some sense "uncaused." This reaction is reinforced by misleading comparisons that are sometimes drawn between stock price changes and the behavior of a roulette wheel. The problem is liable to be translated into a philosophical one. There is nothing mystical or unnatural, however, about the mechanism of stock price determination. It is not governed by a whimsical gremlin. As was suggested earlier, stock prices reflect the results of bargaining among a large number of investors in a very free and competitive market. It is simply this freedom and competition that produces the random movement. Commodity futures exhibit a similar characteristic,[24,27,56] and freely fluctuating exchange rates are not substantially different.[41] Prices of most consumer goods, in contrast, are likely to differ just because the costs of dealing are high and competitive bargaining is absent.

A more specific misunderstanding, which probably also is attributable to roulette and penny-tossing comparisons, is the view that the random walk hypothesis is inconsistent with a rising trend of stock prices. There is no reason, of course, that prices should not rise in a competitive market. None of the statistical tests has been concerned with the average magnitude of the price changes, only with their sequence. Whereas the random walk hypothesis does not imply that any price change is as likely to be a fall as a rise, it is approximately true that any change is as likely to be below the stock's average change as above.

Since the common stock investor is accepting higher risks than the bond holder, he expects to obtain higher returns. Nobody has ever been known to suggest that this difference in returns indicates a lack of randomness in stock price changes. Yet a common misunderstanding of the random walk hypothesis is the belief that stock prices do not move in a random fashion, because some stocks appreciate considerably more than others. However, these higher rewards may merely compensate for such offsetting disadvantages as increased risk. This question will be discussed further in Chapter 4. For the present, it is sufficient to note that the differences in price appreciation among stocks are irrelevant to the current problem. The random walk theory and this chapter are concerned solely with the sequence of price changes of any one stock or index of stocks.

It is sometimes suggested that the random character of stock price changes reflects unfavorably on the ability of investors en masse. This is not true. The ease of entry into the industry and the high potential rewards on capital presumably ensure the supply of at least some very able men. Beyond this, any useful conclusions are impossible, for whereas the notion of a perfect market implies a certain amount of equality among some of the protagonists, it is also consistent with wholly aimless investment by other participants.

It is even more difficult to derive any inferences about the social or economic value of investment activity. The competitive nature of the market might severely limit the extent to which some investors are able to profit at the expense of others, yet the community in general and investors indirectly might still benefit in the form of efficiently distributed capital resources. In the same way, it may be meaningful to judge the value of individual football teams by the proportion of the matches that they win, but the value of football teams in general must be judged by some other criterion, such as the amount of enjoyment they provide.

The random walk theory does not imply that superior investment performance is impossible. It does imply that consistently superior performance at any given level of risk is extremely difficult. The larger the amount of assets involved, the more difficult the task becomes. Since prices tend to reflect all information available to the market and to adjust almost instantaneously to new information, it is impossible to obtain superior performance with the aid only of public knowledge. The only route to consistently superior performance is through the possession of an understanding of the situation that is wholly unique or at most restricted to a few investors with limited resources. This in itself is insufficient if the private information is such as to suggest no more than a small rise in price, which is likely to be the case in the majority of instances. For investors with only small funds at their disposal, the lesson is clear. As far as possible, purchases should be made only on the rare occasions when the investor has private information that justifies considerable conviction in a major change in price, and they should then be made in relative volume. The manager of large funds, on the other hand, is unable to trade in this way without, in the process, moving the price significantly toward its expected level. He must, in consequence, compromise between a lower rate of fund turnover and the expectation of smaller profits on his transactions.

Since the aim of the fundamentalist is to gain possession of private information, the only real message of the last paragraph is that he should recognize the difficulty of his task. The basic challenge of the random walk theory is to the technician. Though his activities may contribute to the maintenance of independence between successive price changes, the existence of this independence removes all scope for profit by examination of the sequence of past price changes. Because this theory strikes directly at the heart of so much investment practice, it would be well to examine the behavior of prices in rather more detail before returning to the subject.

Chapter 2 *Some Possible Patterns in Stock Price Changes*

This chapter is concerned with three questions:

1. What have the differences been between the actual behavior of stock prices and the random walk model?
2. Would it have been possible to formulate profitable investment decision rules on the basis of these differences?
3. Can the divergences be relied upon to persist?

Clearly these are very broad and complex questions. The possible importance of the answers warrants more than cursory treatment, so the most this chapter can hope to offer is some general clues to the solution.

A useful first step could be to review the simple model of stock price determination presented in the last chapter, and then to examine it for any unrealistic features.

The model suggested the existence of two groups of investors. One group, which for the sake of simplicity can be referred to as amateur investors, assesses a stock's worth solely on the basis of readily available, published information together with all that it is believed to imply. Changes in valuation are a consequence of the publication of new information that is not deduced from previous information. Since the cause of each price change is, in this sense, unique, the price change itself must be unique. Thus, the activities of the amateur tend to produce a random walk. This tendency would not be affected should any amateurs cease even to try to assess a stock's worth and make their investment decisions solely on the basis of their liquidity requirements and their aversion to risk.

The model then introduced a second group of investors, the professionals. This group has the time and skill to obtain information before it is public knowledge, and therefore it is able to make a better assessment than the amateur of the stock's worth. The professional will act on the basis that he can make above-average profits by purchasing a stock whenever the current price is below his assessment of its worth.

If the superior information were confined to a small enough group of investors, the effect of the professionals' actions would be a partial price adjustment to the future level, followed by a complete adjustment when the information subsequently became public. If, however, it were known by a sufficient number, they would tend, like buyers at an auction, to outbid each other for the stock until its price reached the maximum level that they would be willing to pay — namely, their estimate of the stock's worth. In this way, the simple forces of competition would ensure that prices adjust very rapidly to the views of the most informed investors, and by so doing continue to follow a random path.

Many of the unrealistic ingredients of this theory derive only from its oversimplified character, but at least one important feature is unsatisfactory.[9] It was suggested that professional investors will compete to acquire stock whenever the price falls below their assessment of its worth. This presupposes that such activity is costless. However, in addition to the costs of dealing, there are certain opportunity costs to be considered, for there is only a limited number of investment opportunities that can be analyzed or of transactions that can be supervised. As a result, most portfolio managers are likely to require candidates for investment to appear to exhibit some minimum degree of undervaluation.

To see the effect that this modification could have on the original model, imagine that all professional investors have identical expectations and require an identical degree of under- or overvaluation before they will act. In Figure 7, the profes-

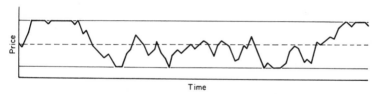

FIGURE 7. Hypothetical chart of a stock price subject to random movement within fixed limits.

sional's opinion of a stock's worth is represented by the dotted line. The margin of profit that they require in order to either buy or sell is represented by the difference between this dotted line and each of the two solid lines. As long as the stock price is within these barriers, it is determined by the actions of the amateur investor and therefore follows a random path. However, if, in the course of its wanderings, the price reaches either the upper or lower limits, the activities of the professional will prevent it from continuing in that direction.

Figure 7 does not allow for the fact that the professional's opinion of the stock's worth and, therefore, his buying and selling limits are also liable to change over time in a random fashion. However, partly because there is only an intermittent flow of information, these expectations are likely to change irregularly rather than continuously. An example of the effect of periodically changing barriers is provided in Figure 8. Even

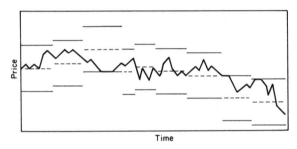

FIGURE 8. Hypothetical chart of a stock price subject to random movement within periodically changing limits.

in such a simple form, this theory has the attraction of approximating more closely than the random walk model the way in which professional investors seem to act. It is also generally consistent with the evidence presented in the last chapter. For example, one effect of the barriers would be to cause prices to reverse direction in the short run somewhat more frequently than in the random case. This characteristic was suggested by the very slight negative correlation found between successive weekly price changes. The barriers could also be responsible for the excess of very small movements that is evident from a study of the graphs on page 10.

If this is indeed the reason behind these nonrandom characteristics, it is likely that they will recur in the future. However, the above version at least begs a number of questions and is not the only theory that can be advanced to explain the non-random qualities. One should therefore recognize the possibility that such characteristics are transient.

If this modification to the random model is accepted, it is possible that the suggested differences could have been used as the basis for a profitable decision rule. Major price movements in these circumstances could occur only as a result of a shift in the whole trading range caused by a change in expectations by the professionals. This characteristic might justify the following rule, which is very similar to the Dow theory:

If the daily closing price of a security moves up at least $x\%$, buy the security until its price moves down at least $x\%$ from a subsequent high, at which time simultaneously sell and go short. The short position should be maintained until the price rises at least $x\%$ above a subsequent low, at which time cover and buy.

By choosing a high value for the filter x, the investor would increase the probability that he is participating in a change in trend instead of merely a movement between barriers, but he would suffer the offsetting disadvantage of missing a large part of the move before he acted. For this reason, the trading rule has been tested for various values of x. The results of application of the strategy to the 30 Dow-Jones stocks for the approximately five years ending in 1962 are summarized in Table 3.[18] The first two columns show the average return per security that would have been achieved for a given value of x. The third column shows the returns that could have been realized with a simple "buy-and-hold" strategy. Only when the filter was at its smallest did the decision rule prove superior to the buy-and-hold policy. The former method would have involved its adherent in a large volume of transactions, particularly if a low value for x were chosen. The final two columns of Table 3 demonstrate just how expensive a policy this would have proved to be.

TABLE 3. *Average annual rates of return per stock.*

Value of x	Return with Trading Strategy	Return with Buy-and-Hold Strategy	Total Transactions with Trading Strategy	Return with Trading Strategy, After Commissions
0.5%	11.5%	10.4%	12,514	− 103.6%
1.0	5.5	10.3	8,660	− 74.9
2.0	0.2	10.3	4,784	− 45.2
3.0	−1.7	10.3	2,994	− 30.5
4.0	0.1	10.1	2,013	− 19.5
5.0	−1.9	10.0	1,484	− 16.6
6.0	1.3	9.7	1,071	− 9.4
7.0	0.8	9.6	828	− 7.4
8.0	1.7	9.6	653	− 5.0
9.0	1.9	9.6	539	− 3.6
10.0	3.0	9.3	435	− 1.4
12.0	5.3	9.4	289	2.3
14.0	3.9	10.3	224	1.4
16.0	4.2	10.3	172	2.3
18.0	3.6	10.0	139	2.0
20.0	4.3	9.8	110	3.0

Source: After Fama and Blume.[18]

The same trading strategy was tested on Standard and Poor's Index for the period 1928 to 1961.[1,2] In this case, however, no adjustment was made for the fact that the investor would have been required to reimburse the lender for any dividends received while he had a short position outstanding. Despite this, the results again showed that the only solace for the adherent of the decision rule would have been the gratitude of his broker.

The failure of this approach does not necessarily reflect on the underlying theory. The problem may be that a large part of the possible gain is lost before the investor has the information to act. If this is the case, a more efficient method is required to distinguish between a price move within the barriers and one caused by a shift in the barriers.[9] This could be done by reference to the midway point, if there were a means to identify it. Though the point could never be known with certainty, it could be approximated by averaging the prices over some prior period. The decision rule might therefore be modified as follows:

If the price of a stock exceeds a moving average of past prices by $x\%$, go long and stay long, until it falls short of the moving average by the same margin, at which time sell.

A similar rule could include the possibility of short positions when the stock falls sufficiently far below its moving average. Both precepts resemble a popular technical yardstick. They were tested on the daily closing prices between January 1960 and June 1966 of 30 randomly selected NYSE stocks.[52,53] The moving averages were for 200, 150, and 100 days. In each case, five values of the margin x were tested. The results are shown in Table 4. In no instance would the decision rule have been superior to a simple buy-and-hold strategy. That these findings may not be wholly typical is suggested by the fact that a similar test of the method on a selected sample of 45 NYSE stocks between 1956 and 1960 produced slightly better results. Nevertheless, the net profits were still inferior to those from the buy-and-hold strategy.[9]

These tests were by no means exhaustive. No allowance was made for the fact that it would have been impossible to deal in volume at the prices used. On the other hand, a variety of possible modifications to each decision rule were not analyzed. For example, superior results might be obtained if on the occasions that the rule required the investor to hold cash, he held instead a selection of stocks with the appropriate degree of riskiness. Although such possibilities must be admitted, on the available evidence neither approach appears to have been superior to the buy-and-hold strategy. The fact that neither decision rule would have been sufficient on its own to produce above-average profits

TABLE 4. *Terminal value per thousand dollars.*

Buy-and-Hold Strategy					
Terminal Value ($)	2487				

Trading Rule — Long Position Only					
Moving Average (days)	200	150	100	200	150	100
Filter x (%)	0	0	0	2	2	2
Terminal Value Before Costs ($)	1347	1411	1103	1740	1817	1529
Terminal Value After Costs ($)	896	926	529	1497	1544	1213
Moving Average (days)	200	150	100	200	150	100
Filter x (%)	5	5	5	10	10	10
Terminal Value Before Costs ($)	1728	1846	1642	1943	1893	1906
Terminal Value After Costs ($)	1572	1672	1435	1842	1764	1787
Moving Average (days)	200	150	100			
Filter x (%)	15	15	15			
Terminal Value Before Costs ($)	1930	1762	1705			
Terminal Value After Costs ($)	1860	1690	1622			

Trading Rule — Long and Short Positions					
Moving Average (days)	200	150	100	200	150	100
Filter x (%)	0	0	0	2	2	2
Terminal Value Before Costs ($)	632	666	374	1053	1103	752
Terminal Value After Costs ($)	26	8	−349	693	687	277
Moving Average (days)	200	150	100	200	150	100
Filter x (%)	5	5	5	10	10	10
Terminal Value Before Costs ($)	1065	1210	952	1343	1272	1283
Terminal Value After Costs ($)	829	949	639	1195	1109	1093
Moving Average (days)	200	150	100			
Filter x (%)	15	15	15			
Terminal Value Before Costs ($)	1337	1257	1142			
Terminal Value After Costs ($)	1245	1153	1037			

Source: Van Horne and Parker.[52]

does not mean that it could not have been useful in combination with other pieces of evidence for reaching an investment decision. However, the author is inclined to the view that such information is likely to serve rather as a distraction from more important information than as an adjunct to it.

So far, neither chapter has revealed evidence of any worthwhile short-run persistence in price changes. On the other hand, there has been very little discussion above of the possibility of longer run patterns. One line of approach here is suggested by the results of the spectral analysis that produced faint but not conclusive evidence of an annual and a 40-month cycle. It is worth testing, therefore, whether there is anything to be gained by viewing stock price changes after the elimination of trend as the sum of three separate types of movement — a seasonal pattern, a cyclical element, and a collection of irregular fluctuations.

It is a well-established tradition of the marketplace that some seasons of the year are particularly favorable for common stock investment. One simple test of this is illustrated by Table 5,

TABLE 5. *Seasonal variation in market advances and declines, 1871–1968.*

	J	F	M	A	M	J	J	A	S	O	N	D	Total
Advances (or no change)	73%	53	54	57	53	50	63	65	58	48	55	50	57
Declines	27%	47	46	43	47	50	37	35	42	52	45	50	43

which demonstrates for each month the proportion of the occasions between January 1871 and March 1968 on which there was a rise or fall in the average level of the Cowles Commission or the Standard and Poor's composite indices.

Certain of these differences between months, such as the heavy concentration of advances between December and January, are rather more marked than might be expected from the intervention of chance.

A second test of seasonality applied a technique for isolating seasonal movement to the monthly changes in the Standard and Poor's Index between 1948 and 1966.[48] The results are shown in Figure 9. This suggests that, even if seasonal factors are operative, their practical importance is negligible. Not only is

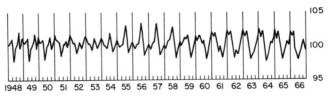

FIGURE 9. Seasonal component of Standard and Poor's Composite Index, 1948–1966.[48]

the apparent seasonal effect very weak relative to other influences, but it is liable to change character over time. Even during the ten years from 1956 to 1966 these changes were quite striking as the summer boom gave place to a summer fall. "October," Mark Twain observed, "is one of the peculiarly dangerous months to speculate in stocks in. The others are July, January, September, April, November, May, March, June, December, August and February." In effect, he was right.

The effect of seasonal factors on stocks in particular industries provides an even less clear picture.[57] One study of 26 industry groups over the period 1954 to 1964 discovered apparent strong influences in the following industries:

meat packing
eastern railroads
air conditioning
agricultural machinery
machine tools
aerospace
fire and casualty insurance

However, since it is difficult to develop a convincing hypothesis to explain some of these findings and since such obvious candidates as soft drink or department store stocks displayed no significant seasonal movement, the existence of any more worthwhile seasonal influences at the industry level must be regarded as at best unproved.

The next step in this analysis is to see whether the seasonally adjusted series of stock prices can be broken down into a cyclical component and residual irregular fluctuations.[48] For this purpose, use was made of a smoothing technique employed by the National Bureau of Economic Research (NBER) for the analysis of economic series. The upper line in Figure 10

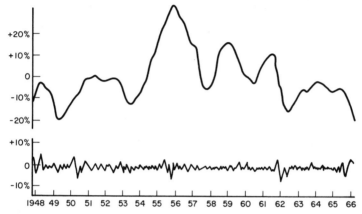

FIGURE 10. Cyclical and irregular components of Standard and Poor's Composite Index, 1948–1966.[48]

describes the Standard and Poor's 500 share index between 1948 and 1966 after the irregular fluctuations have been smoothed out. The lower line represents the residual irregular movements. Visual inspection of Figure 10 confirms the suggestion that stock prices do contain a quite marked cyclical component, though the cycles appear to differ from each other both in amplitude and timing. Visual impressions can be misleading, however, so some assurance is needed that the smoothing process would be unlikely to produce such oscillations if stock prices were a random series.[37]

A characteristic of the upper line in Figure 10 is that a single month's move in one direction tends to be repeated more often than not in the next month. Thus, the average number of consecutive monthly changes in the same direction is 9.8. If, however, the same smoothing technique were applied to a random series, the expected average duration of run would be 2.0 months. Such a discrepancy is unlikely to be due to chance. The NBER has conducted a number of other tests of the method, including its actual application to sets of random numbers. These tests confirm that such major oscillations as those in Figure 10 are unlikely to result when the original series is random.

Any change in an economic series that cannot be attributed to trend or to seasonal or cyclical movements is automatically classified by the NBER as an irregular fluctuation. It is interesting to note that the behavior of the lower line in Figure 10 is sufficiently close to that of a random series as not to offend this assumption.

These stock market cycles appear to have been closely related to movements in economic activity. The NBER has, by a process of inspection, identified 22 recessions between 1871 and 1967. These are shown in Figure 11 as shaded areas. Superimposed thereon is a chart of Standard and Poor's 500 share index. The relationship over this period between the stock market and business conditions is clear. Indeed, of the 22 cycles, only those of 1926–1927 and 1945 do not seem to have been echoed by the stock market. Conversely, only four major market declines were not matched by economic recessions.

During this period, stock prices appear to have anticipated slightly changes in business conditions. Of the 40 occasions on which sympathetic reversals occurred, stock prices led the turn in the economy 33 times, were coincident twice, and lagged five times. The average lead was four months.

A convincing economic explanation is needed of the relationship between general economic activity and the stock market. It is unfortunately much easier to formulate hypotheses on the question than to subject them to test. It may be that the

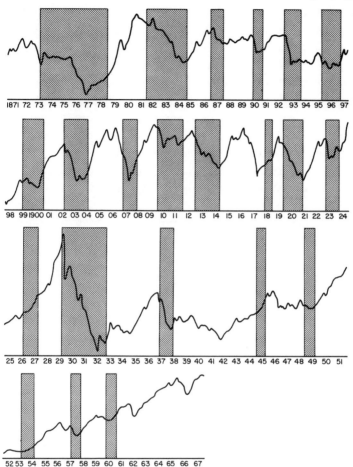

FIGURE 11. Standard and Poor's Composite Index, 1871–1967. Shaded areas indicate economic recessions. (N.B. Different vertical scale for each row.)

market has merely demonstrated prescience as to the course of profits. Or perhaps it has reacted rather more rapidly than other economic phenomena to changes in the money supply. Or the relationship may have been the other way around with the change in the stock market producing a more widespread change in the economy. Probably all that can be said safely is that the causal chain is likely to have been a complex one.

An investor who was aware of these characteristics would have been able to use them in one of several ways as a basis for forecasting. For example, the irregular fluctuations could be removed with reasonable accuracy by taking a two-month moving average of a market index. Since the most recent movement of the cyclical component is repeated more often than not, the investor would then have some information on which to base a prediction. In addition, several economic series have tended with some regularity to anticipate general economic activity by even longer lead times than stock prices. These series include

Change in unfilled orders for durable goods industries;
Change in money supply and time deposits;
Change in consumer installment debt;
Initial claims for unemployment insurance;
New orders in the machinery and equipment industries.

Familiarity with the recent behavior of such series could therefore have improved the quality of stock market forecasts.

It is possible to derive a number of mechanical decision rules from these relationships. For example, the following rule might have been based on the tendency for changes in the money supply to anticipate the stock market:[49]

Invest all funds in the constituents of the Standard and Poor's 425 share index until a six-month moving average of changes in monetary growth has declined for fifteen months, at which point, convert all funds to cash and remain liquid until the change in monetary growth has risen for two months.

A portfolio managed in this way would have appreciated between 1918 and 1964 by 6.0% a year, before modest dealing costs. In contrast, a simple buy-and-hold policy would have produced an annual gain of only 5.5%.

The strong upward trend in stock prices however, has imposed a heavy penalty on those who have erred in attempting to predict cyclical movements, so it is not surprising that there have been quite long periods when such mechanical schemes as the one described above would have produced for their followers less favorable results than those of a buy-and-hold policy. Neither is it surprising that apparently minor changes in the decision rules could have resulted in the disappearance of profits on the remaining occasions. Equally, therefore, a combination of the same decision rule and minor changes in the economic relationship could result in losses rather than profits.

This sensitivity to minor changes in the behavior of the variables could be crucial to the value of such decision rules. Although the investor may well feel that the broad nature of stock market cycles and the relationships to other economic series will persist in the future, it is difficult to believe that they will endure in detail. For example, the changing role of monetary policy in government economic management may well affect the relationship between money supply and stock prices. In consequence, though these cyclical characteristics may provide useful indicators of stock market direction, they cannot justifiably form the basis of a decision rule that alone determines trading policy.

This chapter has discussed briefly only two possible forms of nonrandom behavior. The profits resulting from the application of decision rules based on these imperfections proved to be notably more modest than those claimed by many investment services that rely on mechanical trading rules.

However, it is conceivable that worthwhile decision rules based on these or other market imperfections can be or have been formulated. It is also possible that technical rules and fundamental analysis can be even more successfully combined. Nevertheless, there is little doubt that many trading rules for which the most grandiose claims are made are wholly valueless.

Certain defects in these systems are recurrent. In some cases, the apparent success of the method derives from the assumption that information would have been available to the investor at an earlier date than was in fact the case. One instance of this occurs when the sample from which the selection is to be made is both unrepresentative and unknown to the investor at the beginning of the period. For example, a senator recently gained considerable publicity with the claim that by throwing darts at the NYSE daily price page of the latest *Washington Evening Star,* he had selected a portfolio that would have outperformed most mutual funds over the previous ten years. The senator omitted to observe that at the beginning of the period no investor would have had the advantage of knowing which stocks would ten years later have a New York quotation. Decision rules that assume that the investor is aware of company earnings immediately after the year's completion suffer from a similar defect. In other cases, the trading rule is left vague. Certain apparent relationships between stock prices and other factors may be observed without any clear indication of how the relationship should be used or how to avoid signals that can only be seen to be false after the event.

In many cases, the system may be operable but the profits may be illusory and result from inadequate means of measurement. A common failing in this respect occurs when the performance of the recommended group of securities is compared with that of another group of stocks with different risk characteristics. This problem can be avoided if the results of the proposed investment policy are compared with those that would have followed from simply buying the same stocks at the beginning of the period and holding them to the end. If this is not possible, it is at least important to examine the success of the recommendations in both rising and falling markets. Another important measurement defect may arise from the omission of dividend yield or of such dealing costs as commissions. Correction for this can frequently cause most or all of the apparent profits to disappear.

With a little care it is possible to detect the systems that would never even have been successful in the past. However, the fact that a trading rule would have been profitable in the past does not necessarily indicate that it will offer a valuable investment tool. A formula that is capable of explaining past events may still owe its success to coincidence. The probability of encountering a chance relationship will increase in proportion both to the number of explanations considered and to their complexity. Even if the true causal connection is detected, the world may change rapidly enough to make the knowledge of historical interest only. A decision rule will therefore only prove useful as a guide to the future if it is supported by a basic underlying rationale that gives some reason to believe that the relationships on which it relies will persist in the future. Not only do most technical systems lack this theoretical underpinning, but it is uncertain whether a sufficiently strong theory can ever really be developed to justify faith in the continuance of any major market imperfection. Therefore, although some market imperfections may have offered, and may continue to offer, the opportunity for profitable investment, it is very doubtful whether sufficient evidence can be available to distinguish the true philosopher's stone from the many false ones and thus justify its use as a practical investment tool.

Chapter 3 *Risk—Its Nature and Persistence*

In the process of demonstrating the similarity between stock price changes and a random series, Chapter 1 examined the occurrence of different proportionate daily price changes for each of the Dow-Jones stocks over a period of about five years. The pattern of price changes was shown to approximate in each case a normal distribution. Although it is not inconsistent with the random walk hypothesis, one recurrent difference between the two series is of interest.[14] In Figure 12 the distributions of the price changes of six of the Dow-Jones stocks are shown superimposed against a plot of the normal distribution. Despite

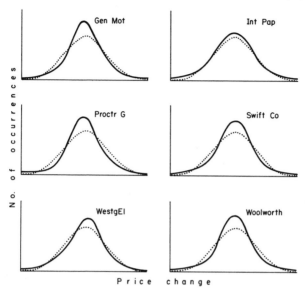

FIGURE 12. Distributions of daily price changes of six stocks, super-imposed on a normal distribution (after Fama[14]).

the general similarity between the two series, each stock exhibits in comparison with the normal distribution a higher proportion of very small moves, a deficiency of medium-sized changes and a high proportion of very large changes.

In order to define these differences more precisely, it is necessary to introduce the standard deviation as a measure of dispersion. This has one very useful property. If a series of observations is normally distributed, a known proportion of them will lie within a given number of standard deviations either side of the average. This is illustrated in Figure 13. Suppose that stock price changes were in fact normally distributed. Then 38.3% of these changes would differ from the average change by less than half a standard deviation, and an additional 30% would differ from the average by less than one standard deviation.

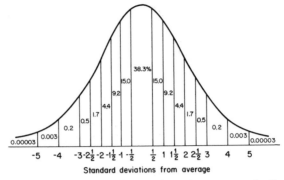

Standard deviations from average

FIGURE 13. Percentage of observations in a normal distribution. (N.B. Diagram not to scale.)

These proportions are also shown in the first column of Table 6. The second column of this table shows the average distribution of price changes of the 30 Dow-Jones stocks. A comparison of the two columns confirms the conclusion suggested by Figure 12: 46.7% of the daily price changes were within a range of half of one standard deviation from the average, as against the

TABLE 6. *Average dispersion of price changes of Dow-Jones stocks.*

Intervals in Standard Deviations	Proportion of Observations	
	Normal Distribution	Dow-Jones Stocks
0 –0.5	38.3%	46.7%
0.5–1.0	30.0	28.0
1.0–1.5	18.4	13.8
1.5–2.0	8.8	6.3
2.0–2.5	3.3	2.8
2.5–3.0	1.0	1.3
3.0–4.0	0.3	0.8
4.0–5.0	0.006	0.2
5.0 and over	0.00006	0.1
Total	100.0%	100.0%

Source: After Fama.[14]

38.3% of the normal distribution. At the other extreme, 0.1% of the changes differed from the average by more than five standard deviations. Small though such a proportion is, changes of this magnitude still occurred 2,000 times more often than would be expected if the distribution were normal.

Although this characteristic has only been demonstrated for daily price changes, the near-randomness of stock price movement should lead one to expect this characteristic to be true also of price changes over longer periods. A study of monthly and yearly price changes of rail stocks between 1857 and 1936 provides some support for this view.[34]

These remarks are not intended to give the impression that divergence from the normal distribution is a kind of deformity. The comparison, however, does serve to illustrate the point that in most instances price movements are clustered around the average. This is true both of price changes of one stock over different time periods and of the changes of different stocks over one time period. For example, in any year approximately 50% of high-grade stocks will provide their owners with a return that differs by less than $12\frac{1}{2}\%$ from the group average, and 75% of these stocks will provide their owners with a return that is within a range of 25% either side of the average. Such figures are very rough, indeed, but they do suggest that, unless dealing costs are very low, the majority of stocks at any one time offer very limited opportunities for even the most able investor to increase his profitability by trading. They therefore raise serious questions about the advisability of a very active trading policy. For the same reason, any investment organization that expects its research staff to comment on, or to generate, a constant flow of suggestions is probably inefficiently structured.

However, major successes or disasters do occur with sufficient frequency to affect investment performance. Again, as an illustration of the order of magnitude, in any one year about one in a hundred high-grade stocks will either halve or double in value. Research effort is likely to provide the highest return if it can be focused on predicting these large moves.

This relatively frequent occurrence of particularly large price changes presents difficulties in selecting representative samples of stocks. This is a problem that is not confined to the statistician. Investors perform a rough sampling exercise whenever they appraise the performance of any investment service. Unless the sample is very large, the average experience is likely to be considerably influenced by the incidence of one or two major price moves.

This chapter so far has been concerned only with demonstrating the relative proportions of small and large price movements. It has ignored the fact that the amount of price variation may differ from stock to stock, so that what constitutes a large price move for AT&T may be a very small change for the stock of a mining company with unknown and unbounded prospects. Yet these differences in price volatility are of particular interest to the investor, for they are closely related to differences in the degree of risk that he incurs.

The price of a stock only changes when investors change their expectations for its price in the future. Fluctuations in price, therefore, are caused by fluctuating opinions as to the stock's prospects, so that, for investors in general, uncertainty and price volatility are directly related. This need not necessarily be the case for any single investor, for he may have private information that is not reflected in the price of the stock; but for most investors, for most of the time, private information is unlikely to be of sufficient quality to shift a stock into an altogether different risk category. The Appendix provides both a further discussion of the relationship between volatility and risk and a justification of the use throughout this book of the standard deviation as a measure of volatility. The remainder of this chapter is concerned with the extent to which such volatility can be predicted.

The margin for error in forecasting company prospects is liable to be greater if either the range of possible outcomes is wide or there is little information on which to base a forecast. The former condition will arise when the concern is, in the broadest sense, highly leveraged, the latter condition when either the business is very individualistic in character or management is very secretive about operations. It seems improbable that these characteristics are typically transitory. For example, most metal-refining companies are likely to continue to possess high operating leverage, advanced-technology businesses should continue to be very individualistic, and companies working on classified contracts should continue to be secretive. If this reasoning is correct and the causes of uncertainty do persist over time, it is probable that stocks that are most volatile in one period will tend to be the most volatile in the next.

Suppose the existence of five investors with differing attitudes to risk.[42] Each is presented in December 1957 with the task of selecting a portfolio. Each assumes that the past volatility of a stock provides a useful indication of its future behavior. Investor A, the most cautious member of the group, therefore includes in his portfolio the 20% of the NYSE stocks that have shown the least variation in their returns over the previous three years. Investor E, in contrast, as befits his position as the speculator of the group, includes in his portfolio the 20% of the NYSE stocks that have shown the most variability over the previous three years. Each of Investors B, C, and D selects in turn, according to his attitude to risk, another 20% of the NYSE stocks on the basis of earlier volatility. If these investors are correct in their belief that past variation in returns is an indicator of the future variation, A's portfolio should exhibit greater stability than B's over the ensuing years. Similarly, B's portfolio should exhibit less volatility than C's, and so on.

Imagine now that an identical situation has occurred in each month from January 1929 through the end of 1957. Therefore, instead of testing the subsequent behavior of just one set of five portfolios, it may be tested on 348 such sets.

Table 7 summarizes in index form the average subsequent experience of the 348 sets of portfolios.

TABLE 7. *Subsequent volatility of portfolios of stocks selected on the basis of prior volatility.*

	Year After Formation	Three Years After Formation
A's Portfolio	100	100
B's Portfolio	137	126
C's Portfolio	164	147
D's Portfolio	194	184
E's Portfolio	244	224

Source: After Pratt.[42]

This average experience provides some justification for the actions of the five mythical investors. However, averages are liable to conceal a diversity of experience. It does not necessarily follow that the five portfolios formed in any one month would have behaved in such an accommodating fashion. But at least the odds are in favor of their having done so.

If, on the average, A's portfolio tended to show less violent changes in value than E's, it is probable that over any one period he would have been less likely to suffer an actual loss. Table 8 lists the proportion of the 348 occasions on which each investor would have been involved in loss. As expected, those portfolios that were composed of stocks that had been less variable in former years resulted less frequently in loss.

These results have all been in terms of differences in the behavior over time of the return on the five portfolios. It would also be interesting to examine the movement of the individual stocks that composed these portfolios in order to de-

termine whether, over any single time period, the stocks form-
ing the lower grade portfolios tended to display a wider diversity
of experience than those included in the high-grade portfolios.
If it can be demonstrated both that the more volatile stocks
as a group have shown greater subsequent fluctuations over
time and that the owner could have had less reliance that in

TABLE 8. *Probability of subsequent loss on portfolios of stocks
selected on the basis of prior volatility.*

Size of Loss	Probability of Loss After One Year (%)				
	Investor A	Investor B	Investor C	Investor D	Investor E
Greater than 50%	0.9	1.4	2.3	3.2	3.2
Greater than 34%	2.3	3.7	4.6	5.7	6.9
Greater than 18%	5.6	6.9	8.0	10.9	14.4
Greater than 2%	16.7	21.0	26.1	28.2	34.5

Size of Loss	Probability of Loss After Three Years (%)				
	Investor A	Investor B	Investor C	Investor D	Investor E
Greater than 45%	0	0	0.3	0.9	3.4
Greater than 25%	0	0.9	4.0	5.2	9.3
Greater than 5%	4.6	8.6	11.1	10.8	14.2

Source: After Pratt.[42]

a given period the behavior of any one stock in that group would
be similar to that of the others, then it can truly be said that
these stocks, individually or en masse, were more risky investments. Confirmation for this view is provided by Table 9, which
shows in index form the disparity among the price changes of
the individual stocks. Clearly, Investor A could have had far
more confidence than Investor E that any one of his holdings
would behave like the rest of the group.

This study was concerned with the behavior of about 1,000
stocks over 29 years. When only the portfolios formed after

TABLE 9. *Divergent subsequent behavior of holdings within portfolios of stocks selected on the basis of prior volatility.*

	Divergence One Year After Portfolio Formation	Divergence Three Years After Portfolio Formation
A's Portfolio	100	100
B's Portfolio	126	127
C's Portfolio	148	158
D's Portfolio	178	195
E's Portfolio	228	240

Source: After Pratt.[42]

1931 were considered, the results were similar. Neither did changing the lengths of the periods over which the volatility was measured affect the conclusions. Altogether, therefore, there is considerable evidence that the relative volatility exhibited by any stock has tended to persist over time. It is reasonable to suppose that this will continue to be true in the future. If so, this characteristic offers the investor a valuable means of estimating the degree of fluctuation that his holdings are likely to exhibit and, accordingly, the risk that their value at any time may be below his expectations.

Chapter 4 *Risk and Return*

A large British betting house, which derives the bulk of its business from accepting bets on horse and dog races, recently inaugurated a new service. It offered clients the opportunity to place bets on future changes of the Financial Times (and, subsequently, the Dow-Jones) market index. Since the firm quotes odds that are expected to produce a profit on the service, the average experience of those who place a bet in this way is likely to be a small loss. Either each participant is unaware of this obvious fact, or each is convinced that his own acumen will ensure that the other man is always the loser, or he regards the excitement of the bet as sufficient compensation for the expectation of a small loss.

This is not the only indication that, on occasion, individuals may derive a positive pleasure from the risks of stock market investment and are willing to pay something for those risks. Yet it is difficult to believe that, in the aggregate, investors welcome uncertainty for its own sake. At least this is unlikely to be true of institutions, most of which receive funds precisely because the individuals wish to diminish risk.

If it is true that investors dislike incurring risk, they will do so only if they are compensated for it. The fact that common stocks have tended over a long period to give a higher rate of return than bonds supports this belief. It seems reasonable to suppose, therefore, that the returns on individual common stocks will also vary according to their inherent risk.

The last chapter described the experience of five hypothetical investors with differing degrees of risk aversion. Each selected a different portfolio of NYSE stocks on the basis of past volatility. Although the results varied somewhat according to the date at which the portfolios were formed, in general each investor secured for himself a portfolio of which the subsequent volatility was in accord with his aversion to risk.

In order to determine whether the owners of the portfolios were compensated according to the risk they assumed, the return on each portfolio was computed over periods of one and three years after its formation.[42] Table 10 shows the

TABLE 10. *Subsequent returns received from portfolios of stocks selected on the basis of prior volatility.*

	One-Year Return	Three-Year Return, Annual Rate
Investor A	9.8%	10.8%
Investor B	11.0	12.8
Investor C	11.2	13.5
Investor D	11.2	13.6
Investor E	10.9	13.2

Source: After Pratt.[42]

average returns realized by each investor. With the exception of Investor E, whose experience was slightly inferior to that of C and D, the investors with the lower grade portfolios would have been rewarded with higher average returns.

Support for this conclusion was furnished by two other studies. One examined the annual returns of a sample of 616 stocks between 1946 and 1963.[13] The other considered the annual returns over the same period of the 500 stocks composing the Standard and Poor's Composite Index.[3] In both cases the magnitude of a stock's return was positively correlated with the amount of variation it displayed. On the average, those who have taken increased risks in their investment do seem to have been compensated by some increase in return. However, it is not yet determined whether the compensation was, in retrospect, adequate.

The return on a short government bond represents the reward that the investor requires for not having access to his money for a period. The return on a common stock may be regarded as composed of this time value of money, together with a premium for accepting risk. It is possible, therefore, to segregate the risk premium for each of the five sets of portfolios by deducting from their returns an estimated 3% for the time value of money between 1929 and 1960. This has been done in Table 11.

It is now possible to assess whether each of the five investors received a reward commensurate with the risk he incurred. Table 12 shows in index form the rewards per unit of risk.

Each increase in risk appears to have been accompanied by a less than proportionate gain in reward. This shortfall seems to have been particularly marked for the more volatile stocks. Indeed, as was observed above, for Investor E the increase in risk was marked by an actual fall in return.

A study of 34 mutual funds between 1954 and 1963 provides some further evidence on the subject.[46,47] The average

TABLE 11. *Subsequent risk premiums received from portfolios of stocks selected on the basis of prior volatility.*

	Risk Premium	
	One-Year Return	Three-Year Return, Annual Rate
Investor A	6.8%	7.8%
Investor B	8.0	9.8
Investor C	8.2	10.5
Investor D	8.2	10.6
Investor E	7.9	10.2

Source: After Pratt.[42]

annual return and the variability of return for each fund are illustrated in Figure 14.

The first thing to notice is that, in general, the funds with the greatest volatility tended to give the highest returns. Indeed, 70% of the difference in return between funds could be explained solely in terms of the differences in riskiness. Since the closeness of stock prices to a random walk has already suggested the difficulty of obtaining superior information for a given group of stocks, this finding is not surprising.

Again using 3% as an estimate of the rate of return on a riskless bond, it is a simple matter to compute the reward for

TABLE 12. *Subsequent rewards per unit of risk received from portfolios of stocks selected on the basis of prior volatility.*

	Risk Premium per Unit of Risk	
	One-Year Return	Three-Year Return
Investor A	100	100
Investor B	86	100
Investor C	74	92
Investor D	62	74
Investor E	48	58

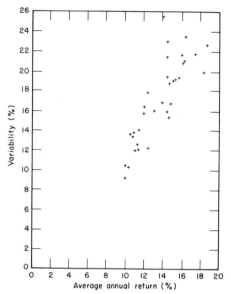

FIGURE 14. Scatter diagram of average annual return and variability of return for 34 mutual funds, 1954–1963 (after Sharpe[46]).

risk per unit of risk for each fund during this period. In order to measure whether the lower risk funds tended to provide a higher reward per unit of risk than their more volatile rivals, the funds were ranked according to both their volatility and the reward per unit of risk. The correspondence between these two sets of rankings was measured by the rank correlation coefficient. A coefficient of zero would indicate no correspondence between the two lists, a coefficient of plus one, perfect correspondence. The actual result was a rank correlation coefficient of +0.44. This provides some corroboration for the earlier suggestion that higher risk stocks have not, on the average, provided their owners with commensurately higher rewards.

What this meant to the fund holder can be illustrated by an example. If an investor had held half his assets in the form of one of the seven most volatile of the 34 funds and had invested the remainder in short-term government bonds, the total risk that he would have incurred on his assets would have been almost identical to the risk that would have resulted from investing all his assets in one of the seven least volatile funds. Yet his annual return over the period would have averaged 1.6 percentage points less than he could have obtained with the latter strategy.

Several qualifications to these findings may be made. The object of investors, it was assumed, is to maximize the return on their assets for a given level of risk. Risk was equated to the volatility of stock price changes. For risk in the aggregate, this procedure is fairly unexceptionable. However, the appropriate measure of volatility is open to some argument, for the choice involves certain assumptions about the investor's desire for gain and dislike of loss. For a wide range of likely investor attitudes the statistic used in this chapter is probably the correct measure, or at least a reasonable approximation to it. The reader who is interested in further discussion of the problem is referred to the Appendix.

Although this measure of risk was employed in the study of mutual fund performance, similar results have been observed when a less restrictive measure was used.[23] On the other hand, for the present purpose, evidence based on the performance of mutual funds suffers from a different weakness. The inferior ratio of reward to risk provided by the more volatile funds may reflect a relative deficiency in management rather than a characteristic of the type of stock that they hold. For example, it may be that the return has been reduced by the high rate of portfolio turnover that appears to distinguish these funds.

Return was defined above as the sum of dividend income and capital appreciation. No allowance was made for the effects of taxation. Since dividends and capital gains may be taxed at different rates, the net return may constitute a different proportion of the gross return for each of the five sets of portfolios. Therefore, if after-tax returns could be substituted in the study, different conclusions might be indicated.

The risk premium, it will be remembered, consists of the total return less the reward that would be provided by a risk-less security. The selection of a value for the latter was necessarily arbitrary to some degree. The general conclusion, however, would not be affected by modest changes in the assumed rate of interest.

There undoubtedly have been errors such as these in measurement, but they are unlikely to have been important enough to constitute a complete explanation of the results. Two other causes have probably worked to lower the premium received for accepting very high risks in the equity market.

Many investors, seeking high rates of return, have the option of buying high-risk securities or of borrowing funds for the purchase of somewhat lower risk stocks. For others, however, the latter opportunity is not available. Their access to funds is so restricted that, if they require high returns, they have no option but to invest all their assets in the highest risk stocks available. As long as no alternative means of achieving their aims is possible and as long as such stocks do not actually offer lower expectations of gain, these investors will be willing to pay up for such stocks. This competition for the ownership of assets that provide a substitute for leverage is even more evident in the overpricing that occurs in the market for short-term warrants.[50]

A second explanation for the apparent overpricing of high-risk stocks is simply that investors have persistently exaggerated the chances of gain from them. This may represent a phenomenon peculiar to the 1929 to 1960 period or some part of it. However, there appears to be, in many spheres, a tendency to overestimate the probability of success in long-odds situations. For example, there is evidence that the odds quoted on outsiders in horse racing typically overstate the probability of a victory.[40] Similar excessive optimism may have caused some overpricing of high-risk stocks.

The broad conclusion of this chapter, that increased risk tends to be compensated by increased rewards, was both expected and well supported. The subsidiary conclusion, that the premiums received on high-risk stocks have tended, in retrospect, to be inadequate, must in contrast be considered one of the least reliable in this book. The suggestion strikes directly at the popular cult of the more volatile stocks. Many of the latter's disciples would be shocked at the suggestion that by simultaneously reducing their liquidity and shifting their stock portfolio toward the less volatile securities they could both increase their expectation of gain and reduce their exposure to risk. The results of the chapter, however, must at least sow the seeds of doubt.

Chapter 5 *Common Influences*
in Stock Price Changes

"What did the market do today?" Such an inquiry usually implies the assumption that there is some tendency for the prices of different stocks to move together. A crude justification for this assumption is provided by the occurrence of wide swings in the stock market indices, which would be most improbable if the member stocks were all merely following their own private ways independent of any common influence.

It is also customary to think of stocks in terms of their membership in some limited club. The most common classification of this sort is in terms of their industry membership. Indeed, the frequent division of analysts' responsibilities according to industry is testimony to a general belief that stocks are subject to an industry influence over and above the influence common to all stocks.

Yet this is not the only manner in which stocks could be grouped. For example, it might be more meaningful to classify stocks into two groups according to the susceptibility of company earnings to monetary stringency, according to the dependence of the companies on military expenditures, or according to their management structures and philosophies. One way to measure whether some such alternative classification might not be more appropriate than one based on industry would be to see how stocks tend to cluster together when the only criterion is the amount of parallel movement they exhibit.

For this purpose, the proportionate monthly price changes between 1927 and 1960 of 63 NYSE stocks were considered.[25] Each stock belonged to one of six industry groups, based on the Security and Exchange Commission (SEC) two-digit classification. These industries were tobacco products, petroleum products, metals, railroads, utilities, and retail stores.

The only aspect of the stocks' movement that is initially of interest is the manner in which certain limited groups of stocks have tended to move together. The degree to which they responded to changes in the market or to events affecting only one stock is irrelevant. It was therefore necessary to replace the original series of price changes with another series from which these extraneous influences were removed. In other words, for each of the 63 stocks, an estimate was required of the monthly price changes that would have occurred if there had been no unusual market moves or events peculiar to the stock. This modification to the original price data was effected with the use of multiple correlation techniques.

The 63 stocks were then paired together in all possible ways and, for each pair, the two sets of adjusted price changes were correlated. The highest coefficient of correlation proved to be that between Continental Oil and Atlantic Refining. One may conclude, therefore, that, after removal of the market influence and individual peculiarities, these two stocks exhibited the closest affinity. Continental Oil and Atlantic Refining were then added together to form a composite stock. This left 62 "stocks." These were again paired in all possible ways, and each pair of series was again correlated. This time the highest coefficient of correlation happened to be between Skelly Oil and the Continental/Atlantic composite. Therefore, these three stocks were combined into a new composite stock and the whole exercise was repeated for the 61 "stocks." On each round either a stock combined with another stock, a stock combined with a composite stock, or two composite stocks combined.

This process is illustrated in Figure 15. Cover the figure with a sheet of paper and then, starting from the left, uncover one column or round at a time. Notice that on the first round, Continental and Atlantic combined to form a composite (indicated by solid black). On round 2, they were joined by Skelly. Subsequently, other oil companies joined the group until round 6, when Southern California Edison and Pacific Gas and Electric formed a separate group of their own (represented by horizontal hatching). Notice the gradual emergence of other industry groups. By round 40, they included a group composed of the four nonferrous metal stocks. In round 53, this composite stock merged with another composite formed largely of steel stocks. Notice, also, that by round 57 the groupings corresponded exactly to the SEC two-digit classification, with the exception of Bayuk Cigar, Consolidated Cigar, and Laclede Gas, which turned traitor to their industries and decided that their sympathies lay with the retail stocks.

In this exercise the stocks were permitted to form their own groupings according to mutual affinity. It was therefore a "look, no hands" approach to the problem. The significance of the

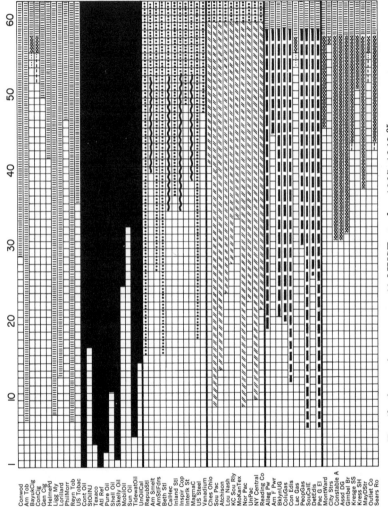

FIGURE 15. Family formations among 63 NYSE stocks, 1927–1960.[25]

results is that the groups corresponded very closely to the industry division. This is not to say that other common influences may not have been at work, but merely that, after allowance for individual peculiarities and the influence of the market, industry membership appears to have been the most important single influence in determining price movement.

This suggests that it may be useful to think of the movement of any stock as representing the combined effect of four kinds of influences:

1. A market influence that affects all stocks.
2. An industry influence that affects all stocks within the one industry.
3. A variety of other influences confined to limited groups of stocks other than the industry group, but including industry subgroups.
4. An influence that is individual to the one stock.

The next step in the analysis is to determine the relative importance of these four factors.

Multiple correlation methods were used to measure the proportion of each stock's movement that could be explained in terms of the movement of any other stock or groups of stocks and that was therefore not individual to that one security. A similar means was used to measure the extent to which these shared characteristics could be explained in terms of a market index and industry indices.

Table 13 shows the results when the period 1952 to 1960 was analyzed in this way. On the average, 31% of the variation in a stock's price could be attributed to the market factor, 12% to the industry influence, 37% to the influence of other groupings, and the remaining 20% of the variation was peculiar to the one stock.

It is interesting to compare these figures with the corresponding data for the period 1927 to 1952, shown in Table 14. In the early part of the period, stock price changes were dominated by major marketwide disturbances. This is reflected in

TABLE 13. *Proportion of variation due to various factors, 1952–1960.*

	Factors Peculiar to Stock	General Market Factor	Industry Factor	Other Factors
Conwod	25%	3%	0%	72%
Am Tob	14	14	31	41
BayukCig	23	13	10	54
ConCig	29	13	3	55
Gen Cig	34	4	7	55
HelmePd	30	9	2	59
Ligg My	12	13	33	42
Lorillard	29	6	26	39
PhilMorr	12	15	26	47
Reyn Tob	23	8	34	35
US Tobac	42	1	13	44
Cont Oil	11	49	22	18
StOilNJ	10	48	16	26
Texaco	12	43	22	23
Atl Ref	9	45	21	25
Pure Oil	10	51	26	13
Shell Oil	19	23	22	34
Skelly Oil	9	40	30	21
MobilOil	24	25	11	40
Sun Oil	27	9	10	54
TidewatOil	15	35	25	25
UnOilCal	19	43	10	28
RepubStl	18	56	9	17
Am Smelt	15	51	8	26
AmStlFdrs	28	32	3	37
Beth Stl	6	62	12	20
CalHec	24	32	4	40
Inland Stl	13	46	8	33
Inspir Cop	8	45	8	39
Interlk St	13	32	7	48
MagmaC	10	44	15	31
US Steel	9	58	9	24
Vanadium	20	48	5	27
Ches Ohio	19	47	11	23
Sou Pac	11	66	7	16
Atchison	12	58	5	25
Lou Nash	16	46	10	28
KC Sou Rly	19	39	8	34

TABLE 13 (*continued*)

	Factors Peculiar to Stock	General Market Factor	Industry Factor	Other Factors
MoKanTex	34%	27%	7%	32%
Nor Pac	20	54	5	21
UnPac	16	42	8	34
NY Central	17	49	9	25
Reading Co	22	39	6	33
Alleg Pw	14	41	12	33
Am F Pwr	22	17	8	53
BklynUG	27	14	10	49
ColuGas	28	20	11	41
Con Edis	15	17	16	52
Lac Gas	27	17	16	40
PeopGas	21	21	20	38
SouCalE	17	24	14	45
DetEdis	34	21	10	35
Pac G El	15	34	19	32
MontWard	22	23	12	43
City Strs	24	18	5	53
Constable A	40	13	9	38
Assd DG	22	37	14	27
Gimbel Br	22	35	14	29
Kresge SS	22	13	6	59
Kress SH	32	18	2	48
MayDStr	23	32	8	37
Outlet Co	35	9	4	52
Sears Ro	20	30	5	45
Averages				
Tobacco Industry	25	9	17	49
Oil Industry	15	37	20	28
Metals Industry	15	46	8	31
Railroad Industry	19	47	8	26
Utilities Industry	22	23	14	41
Retail Trade	27	23	8	42
Overall	20	31	12	37

Source: After King.[25]

TABLE 14. *Analysis of price variation, 1927–1952 (average of the influence of each factor for the three periods 1927–1935, 1935–1944, and 1944–1952).*

	Factors Peculiar to Stock	General Market Factor	Industry Factor	Other Factors
Conwod	17%	34%	15%	34%
Am Tob	8	42	21	29
BayukCig	18	38	8	36
ConCig	18	47	7	28
Gen Cig	19	45	9	27
HelmePd	20	19	16	45
Ligg My	11	38	22	29
Lorillard	18	39	17	26
PhilMorr	24	30	13	33
Reyn Tob	11	44	16	29
US Tobac	22	19	20	39
Cont Oil	5	59	22	14
StOilNJ	7	58	18	17
Texaco	6	56	19	19
Atl Ref	12	51	18	19
Pure Oil	8	56	22	14
Shell Oil	11	56	17	16
Skelly Oil	9	51	24	16
MobilOil	9	58	16	17
Sun Oil	15	33	11	41
TidewatOil	11	54	21	14
UnOilCalif	12	57	14	17
RepubStl	6	69	12	13
Am Smelt	9	68	7	16
AmStlFdrs	9	72	6	13
Beth Stl	6	65	19	10
CalHec	10	55	11	24
Inland Stl	9	61	7	23
Inspir Cop	7	60	11	22
Interlk St	9	60	8	23
MagmaC	12	55	10	23
US Steel	5	68	11	16
Vanadium	10	65	8	17
Ches Ohio	12	59	5	24
Sou Pac	6	72	13	9
Atchison	7	69	12	12

TABLE 14 (*continued*)

	Factors Peculiar to Stock	General Market Factor	Industry Factor	Other Factors
Lou Nash	8%	61%	10%	21%
KC Sou Rly	8	61	13	18
MoKanTex	10	48	17	25
Nor Pac	9	69	13	9
UnPac	9	63	9	19
NY Central	6	72	12	10
Reading Co	9	57	11	23
Alleg Pw	11	60	14	15
Am F Pwr	20	47	12	21
BklynUG	16	43	16	25
ColuGas	11	53	20	16
Con Edis	10	54	16	20
Lac Gas	33	30	3	34
PeopGas	14	48	5	33
SouCalE	10	47	17	26
DetEdis	16	37	7	40
Pac G El	9	46	15	30
MontWard	10	62	8	20
City Strs	14	36	20	30
Constable A	17	51	10	22
Assd DG	6	67	14	13
Gimbel Br	11	60	17	12
Kresge SS	15	41	6	38
Kress SH	19	34	10	37
MayDStr	9	58	11	22
Outlet Co	25	17	5	53
Sears Ro	9	54	18	19
Averages				
Tobacco Industry	17	36	15	32
Oil Industry	10	54	19	17
Metals Industry	8	63	9	20
Railroad Industry	8	63	11	18
Utilities Industry	15	47	13	25
Retail Trade	14	48	11	27
Overall	12	52	13	23

Source: After King.[25]

the very high proportion of the variation that could be attributed to the market influence in the earlier period. There also appears to have been some weakening since 1952 in the importance of the industry factor.

Despite these shifts in the importance of each factor over time, the price behavior of certain stocks has been consistently dominated by the impact of general market changes. Judgments on metal or rail stocks, for example, should have been, to a large extent, a general market judgment. Certain other stocks, such as oil and cigarette stocks, have consistently tended to move as industry groups and could have been analyzed more than most as an industry. Others, however, such as retail stocks, required analysis on a stock-by-stock basis.

The overall figures prompt some general questions about the organization of many investment institutions. The structure of most research departments is best suited to the selection of the most desirable stocks from within any industry. In comparison, the means for forecasting general market or industrywide moves are crude. The relative effort in these endeavors may not be in proportion to the value.

The most important implication of these findings is in the field of portfolio theory. This will be discussed in Part III. However, one aspect touches on the subject matter of the last chapter and therefore merits comment here.

By spreading funds among a number of stocks whose prospects are, as far as possible, mutually independent, the investor can effect a considerable reduction in risk. Since the price changes of stocks within an industry are subject to a common industry influence, one of the most effective ways to ensure adequate diversification is to spread holdings across industries. A limit to the degree to which risks can be reduced in this way is imposed by the fact that some part of the price variation of all stocks reflects the impact of changes in the overall market. This variability cannot be diversified away.

In the last chapter it was suggested that the return on a stock should be directly related to its volatility or risk. The comments above indicate that, other things being equal, a stock will also be more desirable if only a small proportion of its volatility is attributable to the impact of the market. If the stock market is as efficient a mechanism as earlier chapters have argued, investors will tend to pay up for such securities, so the expected return on any stock should be related not only to the volatility but also to the proportion of that volatility explained by the market.

To test the truth of this view, an analysis was made of the monthly returns of all NYSE stocks during the period 1956 to 1960.[13] Differences between company returns appeared to reflect differences in the degree of volatility of the returns, but they did not appear to be influenced by the amount of volatility that the stocks shared in common with the market. This exercise was repeated for six preceding five-year periods with similar results. These findings are open to some important qualifications. In particular, they may have been dominated by a few outlying instances. However, they do suggest that investors may be poor at perceiving and valuing the comovement of each stock with the market. If this is the case, by including in the portfolio those stocks whose movement is relatively independent of the market, the investor may be able to secure a reduction in his exposure to risk without a correspondingly large reduction in the expected rewards.

Chapter 6 *The Effect of the Market Influence on Prices*

In the event of a fall in the Dow-Jones Average, two factors will determine which stocks can be expected to show the least reaction. In the first place, the expected fall in price will depend on the extent to which that stock's fortunes are linked to those of the market. Indeed, if a stock's prospects were wholly independent of the market, there would be no more reason to expect its price to fall in weak markets than in strong ones.

Yet, even if a stock's price movement were completely determined by that of the market, it would not follow that they must move together on a one-for-one basis, for the less volatile stocks will show the smaller moves in either direction. The not surprising conclusion is that, if stocks must be held at all in a falling market, it is wise to invest in those that are not only the least dependent on the market but also the least volatile.

The last chapter demonstrated that the proportion of the variation attributable to the market influence varied from stock to stock. Although the evidence was limited, these differences between stocks appeared to have some persistence, so that, if an unusually high proportion of the price variation was due to the action of the market in one period, the same would probably be true of the subsequent period.

Chapter 3 suggested a similar conclusion for volatility. Those stocks that showed an unusually large amount of variation in one period appeared to be the most variable in subsequent years.

Thus, there appears to be some persistence over time in the two factors that determine a stock's responsiveness to a change in the market, namely, its volatility and its dependence on the market. Consequently, there may be certain stocks that should always be held in falling markets and others that are always likely to perform well in rising markets.

In order to test this, it is first necessary to develop a means for measuring a stock's sensitivity to market changes. Table 15 shows the annual changes in the level of a market index and in the price of a fictitious stock. There is a clear tendency for Phlogiston Chemical stock not only to go up and down with the market, but also to go up and down more than the market. It is, in other words, very sensitive to market moves.

The data are plotted as a scatter diagram in Figure 16. The horizontal axis shows the percentage change in the level of the market index. The vertical axis shows the change in the price of the stock of Phlogiston Chemical Corp. Each cross depicts one year's experience. Either by eye or, more precisely, by least-squares regression, it is possible to fit a line through these points. Two pieces of information about this line are of interest. In the market rose, Phlogiston tended to appreciate a further 1.57%. Therefore, given the move in the market, the change in the price of Phlogiston could always be estimated by the equation

Change in Price % = 1.03 + 1.57 × Market Change %.

This equation can be generalized so that the responsiveness of any stock to changes in the market can always be measured by an equation of the form

Change in Price % = $a + b$ × Market Change %.

To test the persistence of these relationships, a study was made of the monthly price changes of 251 NYSE stocks between 1927 and 1960.[4] Taking one stock at a time, the relationship between stock and market was derived in the manner described above for each of four different periods. These periods were January 1927 to June 1935, July 1935 to December 1943, January 1944 to June 1951, and July 1951 to December 1960.

As a measure of the stability of the equations, the 251 values for b in the first period were correlated with the corresponding values in the second period. The correlation coefficient was +0.72. The coefficient for the second and third periods was +0.76, and for the third and fourth periods, +0.67. By coincidence, a comparison of the values of a in adjacent periods produced the same coefficients. The equations for two successive periods are evidently not identical, but there is a large measure of correspondence.

As a further demonstration of this fact, the stocks were divided into five equal groups on the basis of the value of b in the first period. The first column of Table 16 shows the average value for b in each group. Thus, the 50 least sensitive stocks tended to move, on the average, only 0.43% for each 1% move in the market, while the 50 most responsive stocks moved 1.47%. Clearly, during this period the benefits of any skill in forecasting market direction could have been enhanced greatly

TABLE 16. *Subsequent sensitivity to market change of stocks segregated on the basis of sensitivity in prior period.*

	Groups Selected According to 1st-Period b		Groups Selected According to 2nd-Period b		Groups Selected According to 3rd-Period b	
Group	Average b, 1st Period	Average b, 2nd Period	Average b, 2nd Period	Average b, 3rd Period	Average b, 3rd Period	Average b, 4th Period
1	0.43	0.50	0.39	0.55	0.48	0.55
2	0.69	0.77	0.68	0.76	0.75	0.87
3	0.90	0.97	0.92	1.02	0.97	1.05
4	1.14	1.14	1.19	1.15	1.15	1.13
5	1.47	1.46	1.65	1.42	1.51	1.42

Source: After Blume.[4]

by an awareness of the relationship between each stock and the market. The second column of Table 16 shows how each of these groups would have fared in the ensuing eight years. The extent to which the groups retained their former characteristics is striking. Further confirmation is provided by columns 3 and 4 of Table 16, which report the results when the exercise was repeated for the second and third periods, and by columns 5 and 6, which show the results when the third and fourth periods were considered. In all cases, a strong measure of persistence existed. Subsequently, the whole test was repeated with the groups selected on the basis of the values of a in the earlier period. Table 17 demonstrates that this item in the equation has been equally consistent. Although this exercise was concerned with relatively long time periods, the results would be unlikely to differ substantially if shorter periods were considered.

The last chapter suggested that only about one-third of a stock's price movement has, on the average, been due to the influence of the market. In consequence, even if the nature of the market's influence were known with certainty, it would only

TABLE 17. *Subsequent values of constant a for stocks segregated on the basis of values of a in prior period.*

Group	Groups Selected According to 1st-Period a		Groups Selected According to 2nd-Period a		Groups Selected According to 3rd-Period a	
	Average a, 1st Period	Average a, 2nd Period	Average a, 2nd Period	Average a, 3rd Period	Average a, 3rd Period	Average a, 4th Period
1	−0.51	−0.49	−0.69	−0.41	−0.54	−0.43
2	−0.14	−0.15	−0.20	−0.16	−0.16	−0.14
3	0.09	0.03	0.07	−0.01	0.03	−0.04
4	0.31	0.22	0.32	0.24	0.25	0.12
5	0.57	0.50	0.60	0.45	0.51	0.43

Source: After Blume.[4]

be possible to derive imperfect estimates of individual stock price changes. When the market's influence itself has to be estimated on the basis of an earlier period, the scope for error is even greater. To determine how important this compounding of errors might be, a test was made of 193 of the 251 stocks. The equations relating the price changes of each to the movement of the market were computed for the period 1926 to 1943. The actual market change between 1943 and 1960 was then substituted in these equations to produce a forecast of the price change of each stock over this latter period. These 193 forecasts were then compared with the actual changes. The correlation coefficient between the two series was 0.45. The forecasts apparently were not good, but they were much better than nothing.

Much of the error in these forecasts arises because, with any single stock, there are other factors to be considered beyond what is happening to the market. However, if the stocks are aggregated into groups, these other influences tend to be diversified away, so that the market factor comes to be the prime determinant of changes in the value of a group of stocks. For this reason, knowledge of the impact of market changes can be used with far more assurance to predict the appreciation of a portfolio than to predict the change in the price of any individual stock.

A corollary of this fact is that the difference between the performance of two portfolios will, to a very large extent, lie in the difference in their sensitivity to market changes. This measure, therefore, provides an effective means of summarizing the opportunities and risks provided by a portfolio. As an illustration of this, Figure 17 depicts the record of a representative sample of mutual funds for the period 1945 to 1962. The vertical axis in these diagrams represents the return provided by the fund and the horizontal axis that of Standard and Poor's Composite Index. The experience for each year is depicted by a cross, and through these crosses is drawn a line of best fit. During this period, the holdings of each fund underwent considerable change. Nevertheless, the type of stock held and the proportion of the fund invested in stocks must have remained fairly constant, for in each case there is a close relationship between the annual return of the fund and that of the market. Indeed, in no instance is the correlation coefficient between the two series less than $+0.88$, and the average coefficient is $+0.96$. The differences in the eight funds lie not in the extent of their relationship to the market but in the nature of this relationship. At one extreme, an additional 10% rise or fall in the market tended to generate only a 4.5% change in the return of Fund A. In contrast, the effect on Fund G of such a move would have been a 13.4% difference in return.

It was suggested above that this sensitivity to market moves can be used with reasonable accuracy to predict the change in the value of a group of stocks for any given change in the market. As long as no alteration in basic fund objectives is expected, this may still be the case, even when there are considerable changes in portfolio composition. During the five years ending

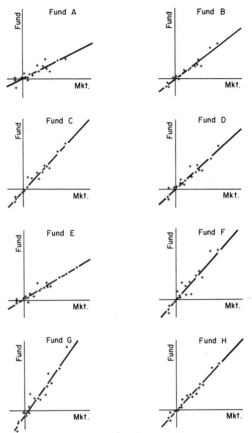

FIGURE 17. Scatter diagrams of return on Standard and Poor's Composite Index and return provided by each of eight mutual funds for 17 yearly periods, 1945–1962.

December 1967, mutual funds seem to have been under pressure to aim for higher returns at the expense of greater risks. Nevertheless, estimates of fund returns over this period, which were based on the actual 1962 to 1967 market change and the relationship in earlier years between fund and market, would still have been quite good. Table 18 illustrates the accuracy of

TABLE 18. *Actual returns on eight mutual funds compared with estimates based on sensitivity to market in prior period.*

Fund	Estimated Return, 1962–1967	Actual Return, 1962–1967
G	99%	161%
F	83	114
C	78	92
H	78	82
D	68	73
B	59	94
E	45	30
A	37	54

such estimates in the cases of the eight funds referred to earlier.

In summary, all the evidence of this chapter has confirmed that, despite the upheavals of the last four decades, individual stocks have tended to bear a fairly consistent relationship to the market. Information on the future course of the market can, as a result, be translated with varying degrees of assurance into forecasts of the movement of individual stocks, groups of stocks, or, under certain conditions, managed portfolios.

Part II: Earnings

Chapter 7 *Earnings and Stock Prices*

It is a fundamental tenet of investment practice that stock price changes are to some degree governed by what happens to the company's earnings. There are good reasons for expecting some connection. Just as the value to a company of a piece of equipment depends on the stream of earnings it is expected to produce, so it is reasonable to suppose that the value of the company as a whole will be related to the anticipated stream of earnings. Unfortunately, the number of questions that can be asked about the nature of this relationship is in marked contrast to the few answers that have been given. Therefore, instead of trying to justify a coherent theory, this chapter will merely offer a few pointers on the subject.

It is a common observation that, in general, the stocks of

companies with prospects of superior earnings growth sell at higher prices relative to earnings than their slower growing rivals. One means of testing this might be to take a group of companies and plot on a graph the market expectation for long-term earnings growth against the ratio of price to current earnings. If the theory is correct, the chart should look something like Figure 18, with the points lying along an upward sloping

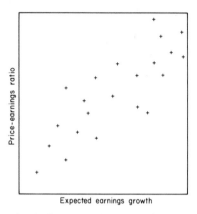

FIGURE 18. Hypothetical scatter diagram of price-earnings ratio and expected long-term earnings growth for a number of companies.

line. Such an approach would be liable to produce odd results in some periods, for the price-earnings multiples of cyclical stocks not only reflect the companies' long-term prospects, but vary with the stage of the business cycle. For example, at one point during 1959, Ford stock was priced at 44 times current earnings, and Dow Chemical sold at 43 times earnings. Yet these multiples did not stem from widespread optimism about the long-term earnings trend of either company. Instead, they appear to have reflected a general belief that the latest earnings were abnormally and temporarily depressed as a result of the 1958 recession. For this reason, a more clear-cut relationship might result if long-term earnings prospects were plotted against the ratio of price to normal, or midcyclical, earnings.

At intervals for the past eight years, analysts at the Bank of New York have estimated for each of 135 companies the earnings the company would have achieved in the previous year if it had been a normal one for economic activity.[54] They have also forecast each company's earnings per share five years hence. On the average, it was found, the differences between companies' expected growth rates explained about 60% of the differences in the ratios of price to normal earnings.

One drawback of this study for the present purpose is that the expectations of the Bank of New York analysts are not necessarily identical to those of the market. Indeed, the whole object of the exercise from the bank's point of view was that it would draw attention to situations in which the analyst's thinking implied a significantly different price from the actual. A related study sought to measure market expectations by averaging the five-year forecasts made by nine institutions for approximately 170 companies during each of the years 1961 to 1965.[11] An estimate of the most recent level of earnings under normal economic conditions was obtained by averaging the estimates supplied by two institutions. In this case, differences in the anticipated growth in earnings were found, on the average, to account for 67% of the differences in the ratio of price to normalized earnings.

A third study employed a slightly different approach.[12] Every three months between August 1964 and February 1967 the utility analyst of one investment firm recorded for each of 56 companies his estimate of earnings in the current fiscal year and of the growth in earnings over the three years to follow. The prices of these stocks were expressed as simple ratios of the estimated current earnings, and for each of the 11 quarterly periods, these multiples were correlated with the anticipated subsequent growth rates. On the average, over the 11 periods,

55% of the differences between the price-earnings ratios of these stocks could be attributed to differences in the forecast rates of growth. This exercise was repeated for another 12 industry groups comprising a further 152 companies. Table 19 shows

TABLE 19. *Average proportion of differences in price-earnings ratios explained by differences in estimated growth rates.*

Industry	Proportion
Banks	69%
Information Systems	64
Nonferrous Metals	59
Drugs	56
Utilities	55
Building Materials	50
Chemicals	47
Food	34
Oil	27
Electrical/Electronics	20
Autos and Auto Parts	20
Paper	15
Steel	5
Overall Average	40%

Source: After Crowell.[12]

the extent to which, in each case, the diversity of earnings multiples could be explained in terms of expected growth.

An interesting aspect of these findings is the apparent variation from one industry to another in the relative importance attached by the market to expected growth. In the case of the steel industry, for example, differences in the forecast growth rates could account for only an insignificant proportion of the differences in the multiples. Of course, the exercise is only concerned with the determinants of the variation between the price-earnings ratios of companies within an industry, so it is quite possible that the valuation of steel companies as a whole reflected in large measure the poor prospects for the industry.

Since no adjustment was made to allow for the stage in the business cycle, it is also possible that prices were being expressed as a ratio of earnings that were known to be unusual. Alternatively, these differences may be, in part, illusory and result either from a small sample size or from a lack of correspondence between the analyst's and the market's appraisal. However, it also seems reasonable to suppose that in industries where very little growth is expected or where prospects are similar, the market is less likely to distinguish between companies on the basis of what are necessarily minor differences in expectations. Similarly, in the case of the more heterogeneous groups, other aspects, such as differences in the degree of confidence in the forecasts of growth, are likely to become more important considerations in distinguishing between these companies.

A little caution is needed in interpreting the results of all three studies. Although anticipated earnings growth accounted for a large portion of the differences in price-earnings ratios, there is no assurance that some related item might not offer a better explanation. Furthermore, the studies provide no evidence of the direction of the causal link, so it remains possible that a high price-earnings ratio is taken by the analyst as indicative of favorable earnings prospects. Despite these caveats, the results do provide some corroboration for a theory that has much common sense to recommend it.

If prices do, in some measure, reflect market expectations of earnings, any unanticipated change in earnings should result in an adjustment of the stock price. To test this, it is first necessary to develop a measure of the expected level of earnings. In view of the difficulty of obtaining a consistent set of past earnings estimates, a mechanical method must be employed. One approach is to assume that the market is able to forecast the change in the average level of company earnings and then bases its expectations on the belief that each company will maintain its traditional relationship to the average. On this heroic assumption, a set of 12-month earnings forecasts was derived for 261 companies for each of the years 1957 to 1965.[7] For each company for each year the actual year's earnings were categorized as either a disappointment or a pleasant surprise according to whether they were below or above the forecast level.

Having done this, it is possible to investigate the behavior of the stock price during the period preceding and immediately following the announcement of earnings to see whether the news had the hypothesized effect. However, instead of looking at the simple changes in price, it is desirable first to extract the portion of the change that merely reflected a move in the market as a whole. Chapter 6 demonstrated that each stock has tended to respond in a consistent way to market changes. This characteristic provides a means for estimating the change in price that is over and above that which resulted from a move in the general market.

Figure 19 shows in index form the average price action in those cases in which the actual earnings were better than forecast. Figure 20 illustrates the price action of the stocks of com-

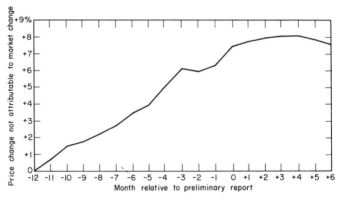

FIGURE 19. Average price movement during months preceding and succeeding the earnings announcement of stocks of companies producing unexpectedly good earnings (after Brown and Ball [7]).

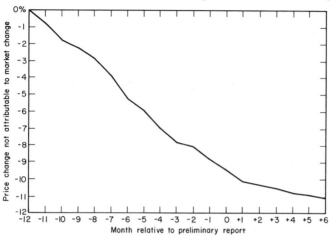

FIGURE 20. Average price movement during months preceding and succeeding the earnings announcement of stocks of companies producing unexpectedly bad earnings (after Brown and Ball [7]).

panies whose earnings were worse than forecast. Both diagrams cover the period 12 months before the publication of the preliminary report to 6 months after. The first thing to notice about them is that their general form is in line with expectations. In those instances in which earnings were above the original forecast, there was a rise in the price of the stock over the period. When earnings were below expectations, the price fell.

On the average, only 10% of the adjustment took place at the time of the publication of the results, and the remainder was spread fairly evenly over the preceding 11 months. This steady flow of information need not have been the case for any single company, but it does follow that, for any one company, the month in which the preliminary report appeared was likely to produce no greater surprises about the year's earnings than any of the earlier months.

The process of price adjustment continued for as long as two months after the publication of the annual figures. This further movement appears to have been small, however, and insufficient in itself to offer the opportunity to trade profitably in the stock.

The two diagrams also provide some measure of the scope for additional profit that would have been available to an investor who was able to predict whether earnings would be above or below expectations. The annual appreciation of the stocks of those companies whose earnings were unexpectedly good was more than 7% greater than anything that could be attributed to the effect of changes in the market. Conversely, the stocks of companies with disappointing earnings fell, over the year, almost 10% below the level that might have been expected just from the action of the market.

These figures are likely to understate both the value of improved earnings information and the degree to which adjustment continued after publication of the preliminary figures. The method used to estimate earnings expectations is certainly very imperfect, so some pleasant surprises have inevitably been misclassified as disappointments, and vice versa. The true spread between the price action of the two groups may therefore have been much greater than appears to have been the case.

A company that produces a major increase in earnings is more likely to provide investors with a pleasant surprise than with a disappointment. Conversely, a company that suffers a sharp reduction in profits is more likely to prove a disappointment. Therefore, there should be some simple direct relationship between earnings changes and price changes.

To test this, 48 stocks were randomly selected from the securities reviewed by the Value Line Investment Survey.[28] The percentage price changes of these stocks in 1950 were correlated with the earnings changes during that year. This procedure was repeated for each year through 1963. Table 20 shows the proportion of the price changes in each year that could be explained in terms of the simple earnings move. Since the percentage change in earnings can on occasion be very high indeed, the figure shown for any one period is liable to be considerably influenced by the experience of just one company. This may partly account for the great variation in results between years. Despite this variation, a significant, consistently positive relationship between price change and earnings change does emerge.

TABLE 20. *Proportion of variation in price changes explained by changes in earnings.*

Year	Proportion
1950	8.0%
1951	0.3
1952	49.7
1953	0.8
1954	3.2
1955	33.8
1956	20.3
1957	64.5
1958	2.7
1959	6.1
1960	41.7
1961	2.5
1962	3.8
1963	6.1
Average	17.4%

Source: Latane and Tuttle.[28]

These results suggest that an ability to forecast earnings changes would have proved valuable even if the investor had no information as to market expectations. This seems to have been the case. The average annual price appreciation of the 48 stocks was 12.2%. If, however, at the beginning of each year, an investor had been able to select from this group the stocks of those eight companies that were to show the greatest proportionate earnings increase, his average annual profits would have been 30.4%. In contrast, the stocks of the eight companies that, in each year, showed the smallest earnings growth, appreciated on the average by only 1.0%.

Another illustration of the value of an understanding of earnings prospects is provided by a study of a selected sample of more than 800 companies.[26] Assume that on March 31, 1962, an investor had been able to distinguish which of these companies would report for the 12 months ending December 1962 earnings increases that were in excess of the average for the period. Suppose, further, that he decided on that day to invest equal sums in the stocks of all such companies. Twelve months later, his portfolio would have appreciated 4.3% more than Standard and Poor's Industrial Index. If, in contrast, he had invested only in those companies with below-average earnings

TABLE 21. *Twelve-month performance relative to Standard and Poor's Industrial Index.*

	1962				1963				1964			
Buy Date	Mar.	June	Sept.	Dec.	Mar.	June	Sept.	Dec.	Mar.	June	Sept.	Dec.
Above-Average Earnings Prospects	+4.3%	+14.0	+12.6	+13.8	+10.7	+6.0	+8.5	+10.3	+15.6	+12.4	+18.2	+29.0
Below-Average Earnings Prospects	−12.0%	−10.0	−9.1	−10.1	−11.8	−12.4	−10.1	−7.5	−2.5	−5.3	−7.5	−2.7

	1965				1966
Buy Date	Mar.	June	Sept.	Dec.	Mar.
Above-Average Earnings Prospects	+31.0	+35.9	+19.8	+11.7	+13.1
Below-Average Earnings Prospects	−4.5	−3.2	−5.0	−9.7	−8.1

Source: After Kisor and Messner.[26]

prospects, his portfolio would have depreciated 12.0% relative to the Standard and Poor's Index. These figures are shown in the first column of Table 21. The remainder of the table shows the results if a comparable situation had occurred at the end of subsequent quarters. For example, if an investor had been able to purchase in June 1962 the stocks of companies that would report above-average earnings gains for the four quarters ending March 1963, he would have realized, after a year, a gain of 14.0% relative to the Standard and Poor's Index. In each case, the stocks of companies with above-average earnings gains sharply outperformed those of their slower growing rivals.

This importance of earnings changes as a determinant of stock price changes justifies devoting the remainder of this section to a discussion of the structure of earnings changes.

Chapter 8 *Earnings as a Random Walk*

Unless an economy is perfectly competitive, there are general reasons to expect that companies with good earnings records are likely to exhibit higher rates of growth in a subsequent period than those with bad records.

Many of these reasons derive from impediments to free entry into the industry. The biggest impediment occurs when the product simply cannot be reproduced by any other company. Thus, competition for Xerox has been limited by patent restrictions, and that for Alka Seltzer by the product identification created by imaginative advertising. On other occasions, such factors as large economies of scale, long start-up times, and high capital costs may impose undue penalties on would-be new entrants to an industry. No matter how convinced the management of a shipping company may be that demand for air transportation will grow more rapidly than demand for sea travel, there are enormous difficulties in the way of its operating an airline instead of shipping, and even if it could make the transition, there would be a lag of several years before the airline industry encountered any effective increase in competition.

On other occasions, one might expect certain companies to pay their factors of production a sum below their worth to the company. The most obvious instance here is the reward to management. If the remuneration of the management of Litton Industries always equaled precisely its productivity, there would be no particular advantage to company profits deriving from its additional skills in management. However, partly because these officers are also major shareholders, remuneration is less than their contribution, and Litton reaps the advantage.

There are many other monopolistic situations that could induce persistence in earnings progress, but the same result could follow from accounting practices designed at "managing earnings." A clear example exists when provisions such as pension fund reserves are varied specifically to achieve a smooth earnings progression. A less blatant case arises when the profit from one effective economic transaction is taken into the income statement over several years, as when the profit from full-payout leases is spread over the term of the lease.

In a dynamic economy with a high rate of technological innovation, dedicated to the encouragement of competition, monopolistic advantages are likely to be relatively short-lived, and new capital will seek out the areas in which the rewards appear greatest. Moreover, accounting adjustments can only be effective in smoothing out short-term fluctuations in earnings. Hence, the first set of statistical tests described below concentrates on the existence of short-run patterns.[5]

The term *good earnings record* has been left undefined. "Good" is a relative word, so an earnings record that is good relative to A may be bad relative to B. Initially, a company's earnings growth will be considered in relation to the average growth for all industrial companies in the same period. One approach in this case would be to draw a scatter diagram similar to Figure 21. The horizontal axis represents the percentage

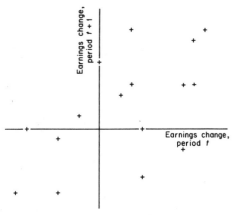

FIGURE 21. Hypothetical scatter diagram of earnings changes in period t and in period $t + 1$.

growth in earnings per share in one year, the vertical axis, the earnings growth in the next year. Each cross depicts the experience of a different company. If the hypothesis is correct, the resulting scatter diagram should be similar to that of Figure 21, and the crosses should tend to form an upward-sloping line. A precise measure of this tendency is the correlation coefficient. If this is significantly different from zero, the crosses do, in fact, tend to lie along a line. If it is positive, the line is upward-sloping.

The percentage earnings changes of approximately 700 industrial companies were considered. Correlation coefficients were computed for each of the 14 pairs of adjacent years between 1951 and 1964. These are shown in Table 22. Contrary to expectations, they exhibit a slight negative tendency.

TABLE 22. *Correlation coefficients between earnings changes of all companies — adjacent years.*

	1952 & 1951	1953 & 1952	1954 & 1953	1955 & 1954	1956 & 1955	1957 & 1956	1958 & 1957	1959 & 1958	1960 & 1959	1961 & 1960	1962 & 1961	1963 & 1962	1964 & 1963	Average
coefficient	−.15	−.04	−.08	−.20	.03	−.01	.17	−.26	−.14	−.12	0	−.02	.03	−.06

In case there is any factor tending to cause a one-year cycle in earnings, this exercise was repeated with lagged years. For example, the earnings changes of 700 companies in 1951 were correlated with those in 1953. This exercise produced 13 correlation coefficients, as shown in Table 23, which again are slightly negative.

TABLE 23. *Correlation coefficients between earnings changes of all companies — lagged years.*

	1953 & 1951	1954 & 1952	1955 & 1953	1956 & 1954	1957 & 1955	1958 & 1956	1959 & 1957	1960 & 1958	1961 & 1959	1962 & 1960	1963 & 1961	1964 & 1962	Average
coefficient	−.04	.09	.07	0	−.20	−.05	−.21	.01	−.10	−.07	−.02	−.01	−.06

Certain monopolistic advantages apply to one whole industry against another industry. For example, it was suggested that airline companies possess an advantage over shipping companies. Other advantages, however, may only be apparent when consideration is limited to one industry. Thus, good management of a shipping company should reveal its benefits most clearly when comparison is made with other less well-managed shipping companies. A good record was therefore redefined as being relative to that of companies in the one industry, and the above two exercises were repeated for each of 62 different industries. Since this produced about 1,500 correlation coefficients, Tables 24 and 25 give only simple averages for each

TABLE 24. *Average correlation coefficients between earnings changes of companies in each of 62 industries — adjacent years.*

	1952 & 1951	1953 & 1952	1954 & 1953	1955 & 1954	1956 & 1955	1957 & 1956	1958 & 1957	1959 & 1958	1960 & 1959	1961 & 1960	1962 & 1961	1963 & 1962	1964 & 1963	Average
coefficient	−.12	−.12	−.02	−.07	.06	−.02	.18	−.23	−.10	.06	−.06	−.02	.01	−.03

TABLE 25. *Average correlation coefficients between earnings changes of companies in each of 62 industries — lagged years.*

	1953 & 1951	1954 & 1952	1955 & 1953	1956 & 1954	1957 & 1955	1958 & 1956	1959 & 1957	1960 & 1958	1961 & 1959	1962 & 1960	1963 & 1961	1964 & 1962	Average
coefficient	−.03	−.02	−.11	−.03	−.14	−.05	−.22	.02	−.06	−.04	.02	.06	−.05

period. The results show little change from the previous ones.

This approach to the problem has at least two possible weaknesses. In the first place, companies recording growth of above 300% in any one year were omitted from the test lest they dominate the results. Their inclusion would probably have produced increased negativity, but this is not certain. Alternatively, since the cutoff point was quite arbitrary, the results may have been dominated by one or two instances of growth of 299%. This also seems unlikely in view of the consistency of the results.

The second weakness derives from the fact that companies that fare best in periods of high economic growth, either because they are highly leveraged or because they are dependent upon such an economic climate for a large volume of sales, are likely to perform relatively poorly in less buoyant conditions. Therefore, if periods of boom have been compared with those of recession, the negative results might have been expected. This does not appear to have been the case, for there is no tendency for the more comparable periods to be associated with higher correlation coefficients.

The first of these weaknesses can be avoided by an alternative approach. This time, 610 industrial companies with a continuous record of earnings between 1950 and 1964 were studied. A company was considered to have experienced a good year's growth if it was in the top 305 companies in that period. As a first step, companies were counted according to the proportion of years that were good. These results are shown in the first column of Table 26. The second column shows the number of

TABLE 26. *Number of companies experiencing a given number of years' growth in excess of midvalue.*

Number of Good Years	Actual Number of Companies	Expected Number of Companies
0	0	0
1	0	1
2	1	3
3	6	14
4	34	37
5	84	75
6	114	112
7	139	128
8	115	112
9	68	75
10	30	37
11	16	14
12	2	3
13	1	1
14	0	0

companies that could be expected to experience a given number of good years if the god of economics had distributed his largess with a pepper pot. The two distributions are not significantly different. Since the manner in which good and bad years have been shared out between companies is similar to a chance distribution, it is a straightforward problem to determine whether, for each company, the good or bad years tend to bunch together. For this purpose, the 610 companies were strung together in random order to form a chain of 8,540 yearly changes, each classified as good or bad. Table 27 shows the number of in-

TABLE 27. *Runs of successive years with growth greater or less than midvalue.*

Length of Run	Actual Number of Runs of Good Years	Actual Number of Runs of Bad Years	Expected Number of Runs of Good or Bad Years
1	1152	1102	1068
2	562	590	534
3	266	300	267
4	114	120	133
5	55	63	67
6	24	20	33
7	23	12	17
8	5	6	8
9	3	3	4
10	6	0	2
11	2	0	1
12	1	0	1
13	0	0	0
14	0	1	0

stances of a run of only one good year, of two successive good years, and so on. Runs of bad years are similarly shown. These results may be compared with the final column, which shows the corresponding distribution that would have been produced by the wanton god with the pepper pot. The two distributions this time are significantly different, even before adjusting for the random element that was introduced when the companies were linked together. However, instead of a company's good and bad years tending to bunch together, there is the reverse tendency. With the possible exception of companies that experienced a very long run of success, a good year or succession of good years was more frequently followed by a poor year, and vice versa.

This test, like the previous one, defined good and bad as being relative to the performance of a group of companies. A different picture might emerge if a company's growth in earnings was classified, not according to its relation to the performance of other companies in that period, but in relation to the company's own performance in other periods. This test also may be illustrated with the aid of the scatter diagram shown in Figure 21. This time the diagram is concerned with the earnings record of a single company. The horizontal axis represents that company's earnings growth in year t. The vertical axis represents the proportionate change over the succeeding year, $t + 1$. Each cross depicts a different year's experience. If the original hypothesis is correct and an above-average earnings increase tends to be succeeded by a further such increase, the resulting scatter diagram should tend to form an upward-sloping line. Again this tendency can be measured precisely by the correlation coefficient. This time, 217 companies with unbroken earnings records from 1948 to 1966 were selected, and the coefficient of correlation between adjacent annual earnings changes was computed for each. Despite a possible statistical bias in the process toward positive coefficients,[55] the average figure was —.13. When each year's change was correlated with that of the next year but one, the average was —.09.

The fourth and final test in this group was designed to detect any departure from randomness. Four companies from the previously mentioned 610 were randomly selected. Five investment analysts were shown the earnings records for these four companies for the period 1950 to 1957, reduced to a common base of $10 in 1950. The companies were not identified, and the only information the analysts were given about 1958 earnings was that the average change of the 610 companies was negative. Each analyst was then asked to rank the companies in order of expected earnings performance betwen 1957 and 1958. Another four companies were then selected, another five analysts were press-ganged, the base period and the length of earnings record were changed, and the whole exercise was repeated. This process was continued until 60 analysts had made predictions for 48 companies. Although the approach of the participants usually involved a general assumption of persistence in earnings behavior, they also paid attention to such factors as apparent response to the business cycle and apparent isolated successes or disasters. Thus, this test assumed much more complicated relationships than the previous ones. The degree of correspondence between the predicted and actual rankings was measured by the coefficient of rank correlation. Only 28 of the 60 coefficients were positive, and the average of the 60 was −.01. In fact, the analysts produced much the same record of success and failure that they would have achieved by tossing a coin. Since they do not in real life base their predictions solely on a study of past records, this offers no adverse reflection on their abilities.

Contrary to the original suggestion, these and similar tests[38] all showed a slight tendency for a good short-term earnings gain to be reversed. It is difficult to believe that the reasons leading to the hypothesis are not valid to some extent. It therefore appears that other forces must be working in the opposite direction and constituting a counterbalance. These may be diverse. For example, an economic system that includes imperfect knowledge and lagged responses can set up a series of cycles as it gropes toward equilibrium positions. However, probably by far the most important explanation is that earnings are dominated in the short run by the impact of nonrecurring events, both damaging and beneficial in character. Thus, if progress was interrupted one year by destruction of the plant by fire, the record would include one year of sharp earnings fall succeeded by a correspondingly sharp recovery. In both the correlation tests there was no noticeable tendency for the negativity to diminish when progress in one year was correlated with that for the next year but one. Therefore, it would appear that the reversal of the windfall gain or loss frequently did not take place until two years afterwards. In the runs test, each earnings change was given equal weight, so a few major extraordinary events would have been insufficient to produce the tendency toward reversal that this test revealed. It seems, therefore, that short-run earnings progress has been dominated by a persistent but erratic bombardment of isolated occurrences.

Time is a leveler, so as the period considered is extended, monopolies may crumble and the forces making for persistence in earnings progress may diminish. However, isolated windfall events are also likely to decrease in importance, so it is still possible that, in the longer run, coherent earnings patterns may be apparent.

To test this possibility, 323 companies were selected.[31] For each of these companies the five-year trend in earnings per share was calculated for each of the four periods 1945 to 1950, 1951 to 1955, 1956 to 1960, and 1961 to 1965. Again, the data may be plotted as in Figure 21. The horizontal axis now represents the trend in earnings in one five-year period, the vertical axis, the trend in the subsequent period. Each cross denotes the experience of one company. As before, a tendency for the points to group along an upward-sloping line would be evidence of some persistence in relative earnings progress. Such a tendency would be indicated by a positive correlation coefficient. The results are summarized in the first column of Table 28. This time, the coefficients are at least positive, but the magnitudes are very small.

One of the problems mentioned in connection with the examination of short-term changes was the varying degree and nature of the dependence of company earnings upon the level of economic activity. On the previous occasion, it was merely

TABLE 28. *Correlation coefficients between earnings changes of all companies — adjacent five-year periods.*

Period	Five-Year Growth Rates	Five-Year Growth Relative to FRB	Five-Year Growth Rates Net of FRB
1946–1950 and 1951–1955	.05	.08	.10
1951–1955 and 1956–1960	0	.03	.15
1956–1960 and 1961–1965	.12	.08	.14

Source: Lintner and Glauber.[31]

noted that even when the two periods were substantially similar, there was no apparent tendency for the pattern of relative growth to be repeated. In this case, a more systematic attempt to examine, and then remove, the effect of change in economic climate was made.

For each company in turn and for each of the five-year periods, a scatter diagram similar to Figure 22 was constructed on logarithmic paper. Here the vertical axis represents company earnings per share, the horizontal axis, the Federal Reserve Board (FRB) index of industrial production. If a line is fitted through these five points, a best estimate is obtained, not of the growth in earnings per unit of time, but of the growth per unit of industrial production. It is now possible to return and con-

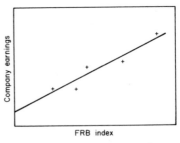

FIGURE 22. Hypothetical scatter diagram of a company's earnings change and the change in the FRB index for five years.

struct Figure 21 for a fourth time. On the horizontal axis is now plotted the growth of each company relative to the FRB in one five-year period, and on the vertical axis, the growth relative of the FRB in the subsequent five-year period. The coefficients of correlation are shown in Table 28. Again, only a very slight positive tendency emerges.

Finally, multiple correlation techniques were used to calculate for each company for each five-year period an equation relating earnings growth to both the passage of time and changes in the FRB. This equation was used to estimate the annual growth that would have taken place given a constant level for the FRB. These growth rates net of the FRB were then used to compare the pattern of growth in successive periods. The final column of Table 28 shows a slight increase in the coefficients.

These last studies seem to suggest that, in the longer run, monopolistic factors survive sufficiently long for a very limited degree of persistence in earnings progress to emerge. However, so far the studies have been completely general in that they have considered substantially all companies or all those from one industry. However, it would be useful to know whether some companies are less liable to the disruption of random shocks and, if so, whether these companies at least exhibit a more constant relationship in earnings progress. Therefore, all companies were ranked according to the steadiness of the growth in operating income relative to the FRB betwen 1956 and 1960. The 64 companies with the steadiest records of growth were separated out and their growth relative to the FRB in the 1956 to 1960 period was correlated with their growth in the 1961 to 1965 period. This was repeated for the next 64 companies in the list, and so on. The results are shown in Table 29. Here, finally, some worthwhile correlation appears. Companies with records of steady progress do appear to have been persistently more immune to the impact of windfall gains and losses, and, as a result, differences in their rates of growth have reflected more faithfully differences in their fundamental strengths.

It may be useful to summarize these results. It was originally suggested that monopolistic advantages and accounting skul-

TABLE 29. *Correlation coefficients between adjacent five-year growth rates of operating income relative to FRB.*

	Coefficient
64 firms with steadiest rates of growth	0.41
64 firms with next steadiest rates of growth	0.39
64 firms with third steadiest rates of growth	0.13
64 firms with fourth steadiest rates of growth	0.11
67 firms with least steady rates of growth	0.07

Source: Lintner and Glauber.[31]

duggery should produce a tendency for a good earnings record to persist. Studies of short-term behavior, however, suggested that any such tendency has been completely swamped by the impact of erratic shocks. These seem to have occurred with considerable frequency, and their influence appears to have been of varying duration.

Nonrecurring events are likely to be of less importance over the longer term, particularly if an attempt is made to isolate the trend in earnings. Despite this, comparison of earnings growth across successive five-year periods also revealed little conformity, even when allowance was made for changing levels of economic activity. Presumably, over the longer period, many of the factors tending to cause persistence also diminished in force.

Only one exception to this jumbled picture was observed. When those companies with the least erratic records were considered separately, some noticeable persistence in relative rates of income growth was apparent.

If these results are to be useful, there must be some assurance, first, that they provide a satisfactory description of the behavior of the companies and periods examined, and second, that they may be generalized to include other companies and other periods.

The tests have been concerned with only a limited number of types of relationships between different time periods, but clearly they are not the only possible relationships. For example, linear correlation techniques were used, but economic relationships are typically complex, so there is no guarantee that nonlinear correlation would not reveal some persistence. However, the generality of some of the tests employed make it very unlikely that such patterns would be strong enough to constitute a serious divergence from the general conclusions.

The companies considered in these studies were not randomly selected, but rather tended to be the larger and more successful firms. Yet these, if any, should be best placed to exert monopolistic power. It is unlikely, therefore, that different results would emerge if the exercise were broadened to include smaller companies.

This chapter has been concerned with only a limited number of years. On the other hand, the postwar period has contained a wide variety of economic conditions. Moreover, a study of British companies during the 1950's revealed a substantially similar type of earnings progress despite differences in economic conditions, industry concentration, and antitrust legislation.[33] There is a strong presumption, therefore, that this chapter is concerned with something more than a temporary phenomenon.

Comparisons with the random walk theory of stock prices are inevitable. It is important to stress, however, that neither result is conditional on the other. In particular, it would be quite possible for earnings to describe an ordered progression and for stock prices to move randomly. After all, the prime condition for the random character of stock price movement is simply that no limited group of investors should have a monopoly of knowledge. Whether a limited group of companies has secured a monopolistic advantage is a wholly different question.

One difference between the two sets of results should also be mentioned. The analysis of earnings has employed substantially fewer data and used cruder statistical techniques than that of stock prices. Furthermore, it has not been contended that either stock prices or earnings describe a random walk, but only that each is sufficiently similar to a random series that the differences are not worth bothering about. Since any pattern in earnings changes offers fewer direct possibilities of reward, a much more marked relationship is needed for it to be of any value. The standards for what may be classified as "near random" are therefore much lower in this chapter than in Part I. In this sense, the conclusions are considerably weaker than those for stock prices.

Finally, some comments may be made on the possible implications of these results. It is tempting to draw broad conclusions about the effectiveness of managements. It could be argued that if there were superior managements, their companies should tend to produce a succession of good increases in earnings. This form of reasoning is dangerous. The skill of management must be measured by something other than its ability to produce a succession of rising earnings, if only because this is partly a function of the base from which it started. Moreover, although there appears to be no tendency for the good years to group together, not all companies have the same earnings growth. Although the differences between the number of good years that companies experience appear to be no more than would be expected as a result of chance, this provides no answer to the problem of where the chance lies. How is it ever possible to be sure whether Xerox's management has just been lucky or whether Xerox has been lucky to have had such a management? Even if it were permissible to conclude that superior managements do not exist, it would still be impossible to determine whether that was because all managements were equally good or equally bad. Neither would it be possible to draw any conclusions about the social value of managerial efforts.

It is wholly false to conclude from this evidence that earnings changes cannot be forecast. Not only is there considerable evidence to the contrary, but this is not a logical inference. It has merely been suggested that forecasts that are based solely on the past behavior of a company's earnings are likely to prove valueless or almost so. The temptation to extrapolate earnings is insidious, particularly when time is pressing or other information is scanty. A study of the five-year earnings forecasts made by five institutions suggested that, to a considerable extent, these forecasts consisted of extrapolations of past rates of growth.[10] A similar tendency seems to be evident in short-term forecasts. It is at best a valueless procedure and may distract attention from relevant information.

Chapter 9 Common Influences

in Earnings Changes

When the wind of recession blows, there are few companies that do not lean with it. In consequence, aggregate corporate profits tend to rise and fall in line with economic activity.

Not all companies, however, are equally dependent for their well-being on a good business climate. At one end of the spectrum, the profits of such companies as auto or steel producers are determined to a considerable extent by their production rates, which are in turn closely linked to general prosperity. In contrast, demand for such essential commodities as cigarettes, beer, and cosmetics is almost wholly unresponsive to recession, and company profits vary with such factors as the cost of tobacco or grain or the promotional expense of new products.

Some attempt has been made to quantify these differences for a sample of 217 companies divided into 20 different industry groups.[6] The annual proportionate earnings changes of each of these companies between 1948 and 1966 were correlated with the corresponding changes in Standard and Poor's 425 share earnings index to produce an estimate of the proportion of each company's earnings movement that could be explained in terms of the fortunes of the industrial sector as a whole. Rather than list the results for all 217 companies, the first column of Table 30 shows the simple averages of the companies in each indus-

TABLE 30. *Proportion of earnings movement attributable to common or industry influences.*

Industry	Common Influence	Industry Influence
Aircraft	11%	5%
Autos	48	11
Beer	11	7
Cement	6	32
Chemicals	41	8
Cosmetics	5	6
Department Stores	30	37
Drugs	14	7
Electricals	24	8
Food	10	10
Machinery	19	16
Nonferrous Metals	26	25
Office Machinery	14	6
Oil	13	49
Paper	27	28
Rubber	26	48
Steel	32	21
Supermarkets	6	33
Textiles and Clothing	25	29
Tobacco	8	19
All Companies	21%	21%

try. There is, as expected, a wide difference between industries. At one extreme, almost half of the movement in auto company earnings could be explained in terms of the overall changes in profits. Clearly, the success of any analysis of an auto company's profits must depend to a large extent on the forecaster's perception of the course of aggregate corporate profits.

For all 217 companies, 21% of the movement in earnings could, on the average, be attributed to the common factor, a finding that was confirmed by a similar study of the percentage changes in earnings of 451 companies between 1946 and 1965.[7]

Such a result offers a useful explanation of a phenomenon noted in the previous section. Since changes in a company's earnings tend to prompt sympathetic changes in that company's stock price, any link between the earnings progress of two companies should be accompanied by a similar association between the changes of their two stocks. It is not surprising, then, that common elements of comparable importance have been observed in both earnings and stock price changes.

Chapter 5 also demonstrated that stocks of companies in the same industry tend to move more in unison than those of companies in different industries. In recent years, this industry factor seems to have accounted for about 12% of the variation in price changes of the average stock. It is to be expected, therefore, that the earnings of companies in the same industry have also been subject to a comparable industry influence.

It would be odd if this were not the case. The fortunes of companies that employ a similar production process or whose products satisfy the same needs will inevitably be more intimately linked. The more homogeneous the industry's product and manufacturing process, the more important should be the industry factor. Thus, a much closer association might be expected to exist between the earnings changes of a group of oil companies than between those of a group of drug manufacturers.

To measure the importance of these industry influences, the earnings changes of each of the 217 companies were correlated simultaneously with the changes in Standard and Poor's earnings index and with changes in an index of the appropriate industry's earnings. In this way, an estimate was derived of the additional comovement that has distinguished the progress of companies in each industry.

The results are shown in the second column of Table 30. Clearly, a large part of the task of forecasting oil or rubber company earnings lies in the understanding of matters that affect all oil or rubber companies. This type of approach is impossible with such industries as cosmetics or aircraft. The prospects of these companies can only be analyzed on an individual basis.

On the average, for the 217 companies, a further 21% of the earnings movement could be explained in terms of the industry factor. This leaves 58% of the earnings variation attributable to neither the common influence nor the industry influence, and therefore is the result of events peculiar to the company or to groups of companies not distinguished by industry.

This analysis has three important limitations that did not affect the comparable analysis of stock prices. In the first place, the conclusions are based on a comparatively small number of earnings changes. Second, although the results support the classification of companies into industries, they provide no evidence that this classification is in any sense the best. Finally, there are weaknesses in the construction of both the common and industry indices that may make them imperfectly representative. Despite this, the results are probably sufficiently reliable to justify proceeding a little further.

It is reasonable to expect differences between companies, not only in the extent of the dependence of their earnings progress on the economy, but also in the nature of such relationships.

For example, the earnings of companies with high financial or operating leverage are likely to be particularly sensitive to changes in the general business climate. Since the degree of financial leverage is usually a matter of long-term corporate policy, and operating leverage is largely dictated by the nature of the production process, there is a good presumption that these differences in the sensitivity of company earnings to economic conditions will not be merely transitory.

The problem is similar to that discussed in Chapter 6 and can be answered in a similar way. Table 31 shows the percent-

TABLE 31. *Annual changes in the earnings of National Steel and Standard and Poor's Industrial Index.*

Year	National Steel (% Change)	Standard and Poor's (% Change)
1949	+ 3	+ 4
1950	+40	+21
1951	−22	−13
1952	−17	− 4
1953	+66	+ 5
1954	−40	+12
1955	+58	+31
1956	+ 8	− 7
1957	−14	− 1
1958	−22	−16
1959	+52	+20
1960	−24	− 4
1961	−22	− 1

age earnings changes of National Steel for each of the years 1948 to 1961, together with the corresponding changes in Standard and Poor's earnings index. In Figure 23 this record is shown in the form of a scatter diagram plotted on logarithmic paper. A line of best fit passed through these points and through the intercept confirms the impression, gained from an inspection of Table 31, that any change in the index tended to be accompanied by a change in National Steel's earnings that was about one and a half times as large. The problem is: Did this relationship continue to hold after 1961? In the subsequent five

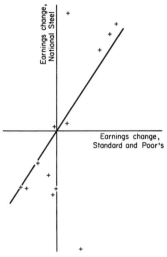

FIGURE 23. Scatter diagram of earnings changes of National Steel and of changes in Standard and Poor's 425 share earnings index for 13 years, 1948–1961.

years, Standard and Poor's earnings index showed an increase of 75%. If former experience was any guide, National Steel's earnings might have been expected to increase by 126%. In fact, they increased by 112%. The correspondence between the expected earnings change and the actual change suggests that the relationship did, in this case, largely persist.

Of course, evidence based on the experience of one company is of little value. Therefore, the proportionate earnings changes of each of 224 companies between 1948 and 1961 were considered. In each case, the sensitivity of company earnings to changes in the earnings index was measured in the manner described above. Then, based on this experience, an estimate was made of that company's earnings growth between 1961 and 1966. To measure the correspondence between estimated and actual changes, the companies were divided into five groups according to the magnitude of expected earnings growth. Both estimated and actual earnings changes of the members of each group were averaged. Table 32 illustrates an encouraging de-

TABLE 32. *Average actual and forecast changes in earnings of companies grouped according to magnitude of forecast change.*

Group	Average Expected Change (%)	Average Actual Change (%)
1	+298	+135
2	+110	+ 77
3	+ 85	+ 56
4	+ 29	+ 49
5	− 14	+ 41

gree of correspondence between the two series. Evidently, there is some persistence in the sensitivity of company earnings to changes in economic conditions.

The fortunes of a number of these companies, as was shown earlier, bore only a tenuous relation to changes in the earnings index. If these companies were omitted from the sample, there should be a closer correspondence between the forecast and actual changes. To test this, the 224 companies were again divided into five groups, this time according to the proportion of their earnings movement that could be explained in terms of the movement of the index. Thus, Group 1 comprised those companies whose progress in the 1948 to 1961 period was closely related to economic conditions. At the other extreme, Group 5 consisted of such firms as cosmetic or supermarket companies, whose growth was almost independent of the general experience. For each group, in turn, the companies were ranked in order of their expected growth between 1961 and 1966 and then in order of their actual growth. The degree of correspondence between these two lists was measured by the rank correlation coefficient.

The results are shown in Table 33. As expected, forecasts based on a company's sensitivity to changes in general prosperity were more accurate when that company's prospects were closely linked with those of other companies.

TABLE 33. *Rank correlation between expected and actual earnings changes.*

Group	Correlation Coefficient
1	+.36
2	+.45
3	+.23
4	+.35
5	+.05
All companies	+.29

It appears, therefore, that the impact of the economy on the earnings of the firm is not only important but also fairly consistent, so that an understanding of the implications of major economic events should be of considerable value in attempting to forecast earnings changes. There is some evidence that analysts are relatively deficient in such an understanding and that their forecasts tend to reflect that portion of the earnings change that is peculiar to the firm. This may again raise questions about the merits of the traditional division of responsibilities in institutions.

Part III: The Portfolio

Chapter 10 *Different Objectives and Their Implications for the Portfolio*

It is a commonly held view that the mix of common stocks maintained by an investor should depend on his willingness to bear risk. According to this view, a broker or investment counselor is a kind of financial interior decorator, skillfully designing portfolios to reflect his client's personality.

This chapter argues that the "interior decorator" concept of portfolio management is based on a fundamental misconception of investment risk.[29,30,51] An investor's attitude to risk should be reflected not in the character of his common stock portfolio but in its size. The widow should put at risk a smaller proportion of her savings than the speculator, but the sum that each is willing to venture should be invested in the same stocks and in the same proportions.

An investor faced with the task of selecting a common stock portfolio usually has a large number of candidates to choose from. These are likely to offer both differing expectations of return and differing degrees of risk. Since there is a tendency for higher risk stocks to offer prospects of greater reward, the available choices, when plotted as a scatter diagram, should look something like Figure 24.

FIGURE 24. Attainable combinations of risk and return with full investment in a single common stock.

By holding these stocks in varying proportions, an unlimited number of different combinations of risk and return can be secured. The expected gain on any of these portfolios would be equal to the average of the gains expected from each of the holdings. However, the equivalent does not hold true of the risk. As long as the outlook for each of the stocks is not completely conditional on the occurrence of the same set of events, risks may be reduced by diversification. This subject will be discussed further in the next chapter. For the present, it is simply necessary to note that the risk involved in holding a portfolio of stocks is less than the average of the risks involved in holding them separately.

The range of combinations of risk and return that might be secured from these portfolios is illustrated in Figure 25 by the

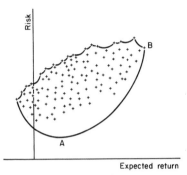

FIGURE 25. Attainable combinations of risk and return with full investment in a portfolio of one or more common stocks.

continuous dark line. The crosses continue to represent the single stock portfolios. Any other point on or within the continuous line can be achieved by holding two or more of these stocks.

It is now possible to give a partial answer to the question, "Which portfolio should the investor choose?" For any given level of risk, an investor will prefer the portfolio that offers the highest expected return. He should therefore not accept any portfolio on the graph if there is another portfolio to the right of it, for the latter would improve his return without increasing the risk. The only combinations that offer no such opportunities for improvement are represented by the portion of the boundary lying between *A* and *B* in Figure 25.

This has narrowed the choice, but the curve *AB* could represent a large number of different combinations of stocks. So far, however, only full investment in common stocks has been considered, although the investor has the alternative of retaining all or part of his portfolio in the form of cash. This cash may be invested in insured savings accounts to earn a fixed and certain return, which is completely unrelated to movements of common stocks. The expected return on a portfolio consisting partly of cash and partly of a mix of common stocks would be a weighted average of the returns on each. Because the return on cash is certain, the risk of such a portfolio varies in direct proportion to the amount invested in common stocks. Thus, not suprisingly, a portfolio only 50% invested in common stocks would have only half the risk of a portfolio fully invested in common stocks. The combinations of return and risk obtainable by varying the proportions invested in cash and any group of common stocks may be represented graphically by a straight line. Thus, once the possibility of lending cash is introduced, the boundary of available opportunities is extended to the area enclosed by the solid line in Figure 26. The question, "Which

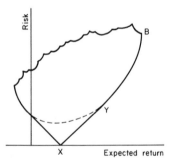

FIGURE 26. Attainable combinations of risk and return with any combination of cash and common stocks.

portfolio should the investor choose?" can be repeated. Applying the former criterion, he should choose any one of the portfolios lying along the boundary XB. But the portfolios between X and Y merely represent different proportions of his assets allotted to cash and to common stock portfolio Y, so the mix of common stocks would not be affected by choosing different points along that segment of the boundary. Only if the investor opted for one of the portfolios between *Y* and *B*, which are fully invested in common stocks, would he change the mix of stocks.

Thus, the introduction of the option of lending cash has resulted in a considerable narrowing of the variety of stock portfolios that the investor should choose from. As a third and final stage in the argument, the possibility of borrowing cash will be introduced. This may be thought of as negative bank lending. The point *X* in Figure 27 represents 100% lending to the bank, *M* represents lending 50% of the portfolio to the bank, *Y* represents lending none of the portfolio. The effect of a negative loan may be seen by extending the line beyond *Y*, as illustrated. Here, *Z* represents a portfolio that would be achieved by borrowing from the bank and investing this cash, together with all the investor's original cash, in portfolio *Y*. Such a policy would involve both increased expectations of return and increased risks. The available opportunities given the possibility of borrowing lie within the two solid lines in Figure 27. As long as there is no limit to the borrowing, there is no limit to the distance that these lines may extend upwards.

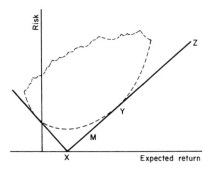

FIGURE 27. Attainable combinations of risk and return with any combination of cash and common stocks, including the option to borrow.

The best of these available opportunities again lie along the extreme right boundary, for only then is there no room for increasing the return with no increase in risk. But the right boundary is now a straight line, and that straight line represents different sums of cash being borrowed from or lent to the bank and the balance always invested in the same mix of common stocks, designated Y on the graph. Which of these combinations should the investor choose? That is a matter between him and his courage. However, regardless of his willingness to accept risk, his mix of stocks remains unchanged, and only the proportion of assets committed to common stocks is allowed to vary.

Chapter 4 suggested that the return on common stocks can be regarded as the sum of two components. The first consists of the reward required by the investor for parting with the use of his money. This is the rate of interest. The portion of the return that is in excess of the rate of interest represents a reward paid to the investor for accepting risk. The distinguishing characteristic of portfolio Y is that it offers the highest attainable reward for risk per unit of risk.

Unlike other parts of this book, the argument presented in this chapter is deductive, not inductive. That is why it sounds depressingly like a geometry lesson. You cannot attack a theorem in geometry on the grounds that what might have been true of triangles in the past might not be so true in the future. Such is the case presented in this chapter. Given the assumptions, the conclusions follow, not just today but always. The value of the conclusions, however, depends upon the degree to which the assumptions parallel the real world.

Those portions of the first section that were concerned with risk involved some fairly specific assumptions either about the investor's attitude to gain and loss or about the distribution of possible returns. The argument of this chapter is free of the more restrictive of these assumptions.[16] It is simply required that the investor seek only to increase his expected returns and to decrease his risks.

Two points of weakness are apparent, however. In the first place, it was assumed that the return on the negative lending (that is, the cost of borrowing) is equal to the rate of interest paid on insured savings accounts. Clearly, this is rarely the case. However, this has little effect on the general argument and merely implies that the investor seeking very high returns should move to a stock portfolio with a slightly higher risk content before he incurs high-cost borrowing.

Second, it was assumed that assets were necessarily divided between cash and common stocks. This ignores alternative risk-bearing assets (such as works of art or automobiles), some of which might have been acquired for reasons other than strictly monetary ones.

The importance of these criticisms is not easily assessed. Certainly, the whole problem is rather less neat than it first appeared. However, these criticisms do not affect the basic strength of the argument, and its conclusions still provide a very satisfactory working hypothesis.

The argument presented in this chapter does not imply that all investors should have the same mix of stocks, but only that they should have the same mix *if* they are faced with the same set of opportunities and are agreed on the odds of realizing various levels of return. In practice, of course, such agreement is rare. Even if they do share identical views of each stock's prospects, differences in the costs to which they are liable could result in differences in their expectations of return. For example, high-yielding stocks offer very low returns to investors with a high tax rate. Similarly, a diversified portfolio is an expensive luxury to an investor with very limited funds. The important message of this chapter, however, is that for any investor, the problem of how much to invest in stock should be wholly separate from the problem of which stocks to own. His willingness to bear risks should influence only the former decision.

It need not be surprising that risk exposure should be adjusted through varying the proportion of assets held in stock and not through variation of the mix of stocks. After all, there is unlikely to be such an effective way to reduce the risk as acting directly on the amount of assets that are at risk. Nevertheless, the interior decorator fallacy is prevalent. Brokers recommend a set of holdings to one client that they do not recommend to another. Conservative institutions reject many possible holdings on the grounds of undue risk without considering the possibility of investing smaller sums in those stocks. Speculative individuals reject blue chips without considering the merits of increasing potential rewards by increasing leverage. The oversimplified lesson of this chapter is probably, in these circumstances, not such a bad one to adhere to.

Chapter 11 *Diversification and Its Effect on Risk*

A portfolio composed of stocks in sound, well-established companies is clearly likely to provide less risk than one composed of the stocks of fly-by-night enterprises. Yet the risk of a portfolio will usually be less than the risk of its separate parts and will depend on the manner in which these risks are spread. Other things being equal, the larger the number of holdings, the less the portfolio is likely to lose as the result of one company's misfortune. It is also important, though, to insure that the prospects for each of the companies are not contingent on the occurrence of the same set of events. Otherwise, the circumstances that would cause failure to one company would bring failure to them all. In summary, therefore, portfolio risk is a function of:

1) The riskiness of each individual holding;
2) The number of holdings;
3) The degree to which the risks are independent of each other.[35]

This chapter will argue that while the first and third determinants are important, increasing the number of holdings beyond a relatively small figure typically has little impact on risk.

As a first step, a hypothetical portfolio will be examined in which the number of holdings is varied while all else is held constant. For this purpose, three simplifying assumptions will be made. First, all holdings in the portfolio are assumed to be of equal size. Second, all holdings are assumed to be equally risky. Third, the risks of each pair of holdings in the portfolio are equally independent.

It is desirable at this stage to quantify the extent to which the outlook for any two stocks is likely to be dependent on the occurrence of the same set of events. In the first section, Chapter 5 concluded from an examination of past price changes that, on the average, in recent years about 30% of a stock's price movement has been contingent on what was happening to the market as a whole. Of course, any two stocks taken from the same industry group would have had considerably more in common than just this 30%. However, since the object is to measure the maximum effect that diversification can reasonably be expected to have, it will be assumed that such duplication is never necessary in a portfolio and that the stocks share only the market influence in common.

The last paragraph discussed the relationships between actual price movements over a succession of past periods. Yet the portfolio manager is, in practice, concerned only with the degree of dependence between possible price changes over a single future period. This is not the same thing. However, just as the amount of past price volatility may be used as a reasonable measure of the risk being faced by investors in general, so the amount of dependence between past price changes may be used as a measure of the relationship between the changes that investors in general believe to be possible.

Given the three earlier assumptions, the maximum theoretical benefits from diversification would be secured with a portfolio composed of an infinitely large number of holdings. If the only relationship between any two holdings in a portfolio lies in the fact that 30% of each stock's prospects is contingent on the behavior of the market, then it can be demonstrated that no amount of diversification can reduce the risk, or standard deviation of possible returns, beyond 74% of that of a one-stock portfolio.

Not only is the potential benefit from diversification fairly limited, but a large part of this potential can be realized with a portfolio of relatively few stocks. This is demonstrated in the first column of Table 34. A portfolio of ten stocks provides 88.5% of the possible advantages of diversification; one of twenty stocks provides 94.2% of these advantages.

Columns 2 and 3 express these results in a different form. The former shows the risk of a diversified portfolio as a percentage of the risk of a single stock. For example, a ten-share portfolio is shown to involve 77.0% of the risk of a one-share portfolio. The third column shows the reduction in risk contributed by the addition of that one last holding. Thus, the effect of going from a nine- to a ten-stock portfolio is a fall in risk of only 0.4%. It is interesting to consider the diversification policies of some European funds in the light of the figures shown toward the bottom of this column.

Yet if, beyond a certain point, the number of holdings has a negligible effect on portfolio risk, the other two determinants — the riskiness of each holding and the extent of the depend-

TABLE 34. *A theoretical illustration of the effect of diversification on risk.*

No. of Holdings	Reduction in Risk as % of Potential	Risk as % of One-Stock Portfolio	Effect on Risk of Last Holding
2	46.3%	88.0%	−12.03%
3	63.2	83.6	− 5.00
4	72.0	81.3	− 2.74
5	77.4	79.9	− 1.73
6	81.0	78.9	− 1.19
7	83.7	78.3	− 0.87
8	85.7	77.7	− 0.66
9	87.2	77.3	− 0.52
10	88.5	77.0	− 0.42
11	89.5	76.7	− 0.35
12	90.4	76.5	− 0.29
13	91.1	76.3	− 0.25
14	91.7	76.2	− 0.21
15	92.3	76.0	− 0.19
16	92.7	75.9	− 0.16
17	93.2	75.8	− 0.14
18	93.5	75.7	− 0.13
19	93.9	75.6	− 0.12
20	94.2	75.5	− 0.10
30	96.1	75.0	− 0.05
50	97.7	74.6	− 0.02
100	98.83	74.31	− 0.0041
500	99.76	74.07	− 0.0002
1,000	99.88	74.04	− 0.00004
2,000	99.94	74.02	− 0.00001

ence between these risks — are both important. Reduce the risk of the individual holdings by so much, and the portfolio risk is reduced in the same proportion. The effect of holding securities whose fortunes are less dependent on the same circumstances is more complex and can best be illustrated by an example. The first column of Table 35 is extracted from Table 34. It shows the reduction in risk that would be achieved with varying degrees of diversification, given that 30% of the outlook for a group of stocks is dependent on the occurrence of the same set

TABLE 35. *A theoretical illustration of the effect on risk of holding stocks with less interrelated prospects.*

Number of Holdings	Risk as % of One-Stock Portfolio, Group 1	Risk as % of One-Stock Portfolio, Group 2
2	88.0%	86.6%
3	83.6	81.6
4	81.3	79.1
5	79.9	77.5
6	78.9	76.4
7	78.3	75.6
8	77.7	75.0
9	77.3	74.5
10	77.0	74.2
11	76.7	73.9
12	76.5	73.6
13	76.3	73.4
14	76.2	73.2
15	76.0	73.0
16	75.9	72.9
17	75.8	72.8
18	75.7	72.6
19	75.6	72.5
20	75.5	72.5
30	75.0	71.9
50	74.6	71.4
100	74.31	71.06
500	74.07	70.78
1,000	74.04	70.75
2,000	74.02	70.73

of events. In the second column of Table 35, this assumption has been changed so that only 25% of the outlook is conditional on the same events. A portfolio of ten securities formed from this second group of stocks would have 3.7% less risk than a ten-security portfolio formed from the original group. Perhaps a more striking demonstration that the quality of the diversification is more important than the quantity is the fact that an eleven-security portfolio drawn from the second group would be less risky than a 2,000-stock portfolio formed from the first.

A somewhat less artificial, if less precise, demonstration of the progressively diminishing effects of diversification is provided by a study of the stocks of 140 large corporations.[19] From this sample, five portfolios, each consisting of just three stocks, were selected at random. This exercise was repeated six times; on each successive occasion, the portfolios comprised a larger number of holdings. The volatility of the monthly returns of each portfolio was computed for the period 1960 to 1963. Table 36 provides a summary of the results. On the average, the vola-

TABLE 36. *An empirical illustration of the effect of diversification on risk.*

Number of Holdings	3	6	11	18	26	36	44
Average Risk of Five Portfolios*	126	112	107	105	101	105	107

* Expressed as % of risk of 140-stock portfolio.

tility of the five least diversified portfolios was 26% greater than that of a portfolio composed of all 140 stocks. However, as the number of holdings was increased, the avoidable risk diminished rapidly. Indeed, beyond about 18 holdings, the degree of diversification seems to be a far less important consideration than which stocks came out of the hat.

These examples demonstrate generally that increasing diversification beyond a certain point is unlikely to be an effective way of reducing exposure to risk. They suffer, however, from the artificiality embodied in their assumptions. One such limitation stems from the supposition that holdings are always equal in size. Usually this neither is, nor ought to be, the case. Yet if the risks are not spread evenly, a larger number of holdings is required to achieve the same reduction.

The other assumptions constitute a more serious drawback.

Thus, all stocks are not equally risky, as the simple model suggested. If an increase in the number of holdings involved the addition of higher risk securities, the net effect could be an increase rather than a fall in risk. In a similar way, all stocks are not equally independent. For example, stocks within the same industry group have more in common than stocks from different industries. In consequence, increasing the number of holdings is likely to prove far less effective when it reaches the stage of duplicating representation in an industry. The force of these remarks is that whereas the above examples could demonstrate that diversification beyond about 20 securities cannot reduce risk by a meaningful amount, they were unable to provide information as to whether such diversification, in practice, offers any reduction in risk at all. What is needed is some indication of the stage at which the benefits of increasing diversification typically begin to be outweighed by the concomitant disadvantages. In other words, it would be useful to know how many securities are likely to be held in a portfolio that is constructed to minimize risk.

Given a measure of the risk of the eligible stocks and of the relationship between each pair of stocks, there are straightforward mathematical techniques for determining the composition of this minimum-risk portfolio. The problem is to determine these quantities. One method is to ask the investor to describe, either directly or indirectly, his degree of conviction about each stock's prospects and the relationships between these prospects. Whenever this has been tried, the computed minimum-risk portfolio has typically consisted of no more than five holdings. The objection to this approach is that there is no assurance that the investor is describing his beliefs accurately. Therefore, it is probably more appropriate to base the computations on historical data and to assume that risk is directly proportional to the degree of volatility and that the dependence between possible price changes over a single time period is equal to the dependence between actual price changes over a number of periods.

To this end, a representative sample of 100 NYSE stocks was selected. Measures of individual risk and dependence were calculated from the monthly price changes between 1963 and 1967. Of all the possible portfolios that could have been selected from these 100 stocks, the portfolio with the least risk consisted of just 15 holdings.

This result is the more striking when considered in conjunction with the conclusion of the last chapter. It was argued there that an investor should only be interested in selecting from a short list of possible candidates, which are represented as lying along the line AB in Figure 25. The characteristic shared by each of these candidates is that no other portfolio can be constructed to offer as little risk for a given level of return. The portfolio with the least possible risk is represented by point A, and of all the candidates for the investor's consideration, this portfolio contains the largest number of holdings. The stock portfolio in the example above is therefore the most diversified of the short list candidates. Whether the investor should choose this portfolio or one with an even smaller number of holdings would depend upon which offered the highest reward for risk per unit of risk.

Only if the investor considers that the risks of stocks are far less interrelated than their past history indicates should he be willing to accept a much larger number of holdings than the example suggests.

The assumptions behind the measure of risk adopted throughout this book are discussed in the Appendix. The one that is most open to criticism is that stock price changes can be treated as if they were normally distributed. In this instance, allowance for the departures from normality that were described at the beginning of Chapter 3 would probably reduce even further the extent to which risks can be avoided by diversification.[15]

The futility of multiplying the number of holdings in a portfolio is therefore one of the most reliable lessons of this book.

This does not imply that a portfolio manager will at any time be able to maintain the optimum number of holdings. For example, he may be prevented from doing so by legal restrictions. Furthermore, large holdings are seldom acquired or sold instantaneously, so the number of holdings may often be inflated by the existence of some that are in the process of liquidation. Alternatively, lack of marketability for a stock may make it impossible ever to obtain as large a holding as might otherwise be desirable. Targets, however, are no less targets because they cannot always be hit.

For both the individual and the corporate investor this chapter should provide some lessons. It has been estimated that the average number of stocks directly owned by the individual investor is between three and four.[32] It can be shown that, given some degree of uncertainty on the part of the investor and a choice of securities whose returns are imperfectly correlated, it will always pay to own more than one security.[44] This chapter has argued that the benefits of diversification will usually continue to accrue at least beyond three or four holdings. A large number of the portfolios of individual investors are therefore inadequately diversified.

One of the advantages claimed by investment institutions is that they provide the only opportunity for individuals to gain the full benefit of diversification. While such an argument has much to recommend it, the number of holdings necessary to achieve an optimum amount of diversification may not be out of the reach of many individual investors.

If most individual investors own too few holdings, the reverse usually holds true of institutions. The benefits that they gain from their large number of holdings are at best minimal and are probably more than outweighed by the inclusion of securities that offer lower expectations of reward per unit of risk.

Appendix The Assumptions Behind the
*Use of the Standard Deviation of
Past Returns as a Measure of Risk*

The purpose of this Appendix is to explain in rather more detail the assumptions underlying the use of the standard deviation of actual price changes as a measure of risk.

The first part of the argument requires a general theory of the behavior of individuals under uncertainty.[22,39] Early works on behavior under uncertainty suggested that economic man is concerned solely with maximizing the expected monetary gain from any undertaking. This "expected gain" is defined as the

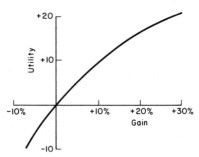

FIGURE A.1. Utility curve with diminishing marginal utility of wealth.

sum of all possible outcomes, each weighted by the probability of occurrence. Thus, a stock that promised a 50% chance of a 5% loss and a 50% chance of a 15% gain would have an expected return of 50% × −5% + 50% × 15%, or 5%. It is the expected gain in the sense that if the investor keeps playing the averages, he can expect over the long run to receive this return. Many human actions, however, can be shown to be inconsistent with the expected monetary return principle. Any investor who adheres to it should be indifferent about two stocks that offer the same expected return. Yet, in practice, investors are unlikely to regard with equal favor the investment described above and a stock that offers equal chances of a 100% loss and a 110% gain.

Realization of these limitations led to the proposal of a different explanation of human behavior based on the maximization of expected utility. This principle has been stated in many forms. The crude version that follows was adopted by the author on the grounds of its immediate plausibility rather than its logical coherence.

The horizontal axis of Figure A.1 records a variety of possible outcomes from an investment. The vertical axis measures the degree of satisfaction or utility attaching to each payoff. A zero gain has been defined as providing zero units of satisfaction, and a 10% gain as providing 10 units of satisfaction. The numbers attaching to these two reference points are arbitrary in the same way that the boiling and freezing points on the Fahrenheit scale are arbitrary. However, once these points have been fixed, it is possible to determine the utility attaching to other outcomes. To most individuals, money has a diminishing marginal utility, so a gain of $100 imparts less than twice the satisfaction of a gain of $50. For this reason, the utility curve is typically of the rainbow shape shown in Figure A.1. Instead of maximizing the expected gain, the investor is assumed to seek to maximize the expected satisfaction from any action. Consider the hypothetical investment suggested earlier, which had a 50% chance of a 5% loss and a 50% chance of a 15% gain. Figure A.1 shows that a 5% loss would cause $-6\frac{1}{2}$ units of satisfaction, and a 15% profit, $+13\frac{1}{2}$ units. Since the two events are equally likely to occur, the expected utility from such an investment lies midway between these figures at $+3\frac{1}{2}$ units. Figure A.1 also shows that the same amount of satisfaction could have been provided by an investment with a certain return of just under $3\frac{1}{2}$%. Thus, despite the fact that the two investments offer different expected monetary returns, the investor is indifferent which he holds.

The rainbow of Figure A.1 describes the preferences of the risk averter, but it is not the only shape the utility curve could describe. In Figure A.2 the curve is saucer-like. This is the

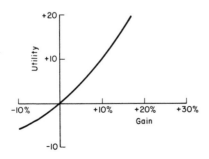

FIGURE A.2. Utility curve with increasing marginal utility of wealth.

curve of the gambler who likes taking risk for risk's sake. An individual with such a curve would always prefer an even gamble of making or losing $100 to doing nothing.

In Figure A.3, the utility function is shown by a straight line.

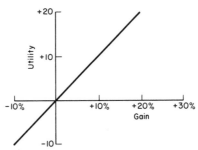

FIGURE A.3. Utility curve with constant marginal utility of wealth.

Such an individual would neither seek nor avoid risk: he would merely be indifferent to it. He would therefore regard doing nothing and even chances of making or losing $100 as equally attractive.

The conditions implied by the utility curves of Figure A.2 and A.3 are likely to be rare in individuals. It is doubtful whether an institution ever can, or should, adopt such a set of preferences. The treatment of risk throughout this book involves the basic assumption that money possesses a diminishing marginal utility and therefore that the investor's utility curve is arched as in Figure A.1.

The use of the standard deviation of possible outcomes as a measure of risk unfortunately involves more specific assumptions than just that the utility curve should be arched.[29,30,35] At least one of two further conditions must be satisfied. The first of these conditions requires that the utility curve be definable by a quadratic equation, an example of which is shown in Figure A.4. The first part of this curve resembles that of Figure A.1. However, a quadratic curve must begin to decline

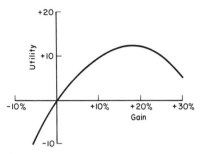

FIGURE A.4. Quadratic utility curve.

again at some point. This would imply that there is some point at which the investor would prefer to have less, rather than more money — an uncommon characteristic. However, it may be that over the range of gains that the investor can realistically hope for, his utility curve is very similar to a quadratic curve and that the point at which the quadratic curve fails to describe his wishes is so far along the base line that it is irrelevant to practical decision-making anyway. How close the condition comes to being satisfied it is very difficult to judge, if only because individuals find it difficult to provide the information necessary to determine their utility function. The approximation may be quite good for less risk-conscious investors, but is probably unsatisfactory for those with rapidly diminishing marginal utility.

It is not necessary, however, that the investor's utility curve be quadratic in form, so long as a second condition is satisfied. This condition requires that the possible changes in the value of the portfolios involved conform to a normal distribution, such as is the case in Figure A.5. Chapter 1 suggested that the distribution of price changes that actually occurs is very similar to a normal distribution, although some important differences were pointed out in Chapter 3. Yet if the various price changes that have occurred in the past were normally distributed, it is still possible that the investor might view the future in a different light. However, the divergences from the normal dis-

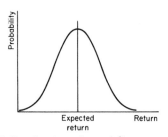

FIGURE A.5. Normal distribution of portfolio returns.

tribution for single stocks would tend to cancel out when the whole portfolio was considered. In sum, it seems unlikely that the second condition is ever fully satisfied, but on the other hand, the approximation is probably sufficiently close to be useful.

Ignoring, then, the possibility of the first condition being met, the use of the standard deviation of possible outcomes as a measure of risk can be justified as long as the investor's utility curve is arched and the distribution of portfolio outcomes is normal. It is sometimes suggested that the standard deviation cannot be the appropriate measure of risk, because the risk lies only in the possibility that the gain will fall short of the expected return, whereas the magnitude of the standard deviation is affected by observations both above and below the expected level. However, if the normality condition is satisfied, the section of the distribution lying above the expected return is a mirror image of the section below. The standard deviation, therefore, can, in this case, equally well be thought of as merely measuring the chances of a shortfall from the expected outcome.

The preceding paragraphs have shown that risk lies in the amount of variation in possible outcomes and that under certain assumptions the appropriate measure of this variation is the standard deviation. It is still necessary to demonstrate the relationship with price volatility.

Imagine that an investor had impeccable information about

the volatility of a stock over the following year. For example, he might know that half the daily price changes of Explosive Corporation of America would consist of a rise of 2% and the other half would involve a fall of 2%. If he had no further information as to the outlook for Explosive Corporation stock, the investor would assume not only that tomorrow's price change must be either a rise or a fall of 2%, but that the odds of it being one or the other are exactly 50–50. In other words, where no information on the sequence of price changes is available, the odds of any given change occurring on an occasion are equivalent to the frequency with which that change occurs over time. In such circumstances, the standard deviation of actual price changes over consecutive periods is equal to the standard deviation of possible price changes over a single period.

The critical condition for this equality is contained in the clause, "where no information on the sequence of price changes is available." Clearly, if the investor in the example had also known that the next day's price change was going to be a rise, there would be no variation in possible outcomes, and the standard deviation of successive price changes would be a very bad measure of risk.

Chapters 1 and 2 argued that private information about a stock's prospects must be very restricted in distribution or trival in content for it not to be reflected already in price. Special information clearly does occur, but it is very doubtful whether it is of sufficient quality, sufficiently often, to affect greatly a stock's relative riskiness. Yet even if the reader is unconvinced by this suggestion, volatility can still be valuable as a measure of the risk that is inherent in the stock before its prospects are investigated. If professional analysis is able to effect the same *proportionate* reduction of risk for volatile and nonvolatile stocks, the conclusions in this book based on the use of volatility are still meaningful.

Company Names and Abbreviations

The following is a listing of companies referred to in this book, together with the abbreviations used for them in tables and figures.

Company	*Abbreviation*
Allegheny Power System, Inc.	AllegPw
Allied Chemical Corporation	AlliedCh
Aluminum Company of America	Alcoa
American Can Company	Am Can
American & Foreign Power Company, Inc.	Am F Pwr
American Smelting and Refining Company	Am Smelt
American Steel Foundries	AmStlFdrs
American Telephone & Telegraph Company	AmT&T
The American Tobacco Company	Am Tob
Anaconda Company	Anacond
Associated Dry Goods Corporation	Assd DG

Company	*Abbreviation*
The Atchison, Topeka & Santa Fe Railway Company	Atchison
Atlantic Refining Co.	Atl Ref
Bayuk Cigars Incorporated	BayukCig
Bethlehem Steel Corporation	Beth Stl
The Brooklyn Union Gas Company	BklynUG
Calumet & Hecla, Inc.	CalHec
The Chesapeake and Ohio Railway Company	Ches Ohio
Chrysler Corporation	Chrysler
City Stores Company	City Strs
The Columbia Gas System, Inc.	ColuGas
Consolidated Cigar Corp.	Con Cig
Consolidated Edison Company of New York, Inc.	Con Edis
Arnold Constable Corp.	Constable A
Continental Oil Company	Cont Oil
Conwood Corp. (formerly American Snuff Co.)	Conwod
Detroit Edison Company	DetEdis
E. I. duPont de Nemours & Company	duPont
Eastman Kodak Company	E Kodak
General Cigar Co., Inc.	Gen Cig
General Electric Company	Gen Elec
General Foods Corporation	Gen Fds
General Motors Corporation	GenMot
Gimbel Brothers, Inc.	Gimbel Br
Goodyear Tire & Rubber Company	Goodyr
Helme Products, Inc.	HelmePd
Inland Steel Company	Inland Stl
Inspiration Consolidated Copper Company	Inspir Cop
Interlake Steel Corporation (formerly Interlake Iron Corporation)	InterlkSt
International Harvester Company	Int Harv
International Nickel Company of Canada, Ltd.	Int Nick
International Paper Company	Int Pap
Johns-Manville Corporation	JohnMan
The Kansas City Southern Railway Company	KC Sou Rly
S. S. Kresge Company	Kresge SS
S. H. Kress & Co.	Kress SH

Company	Abbreviation
Laclede Gas Company	Lac Gas
Liggett & Myers Incorporated	Ligg My
Litton Industries, Inc.	Litton Ind
Lorillard Corporation	Lorillard
Louisville & Nashville Railroad Co.	Lou Nash
Magma Copper Co.	MagmaC
The May Department Stores Company	MayDStr
Missouri-Kansas-Texas Railroad Company	MoKanTex
Mobil Oil Corporation	MobilOil
Montgomery Ward & Co., Incorporated	MontWard
National Steel Corporation	Nat Steel
New York Central Railroad Company	NY Central
Northern Pacific Railway Company	Nor Pac
Outlet Co.	Outlet Co
Owens-Illinois, Inc.	OwensIll
Pacific Gas & Electric Company	Pac G El
Peoples Gas System, Inc.	PeopGas
Philip Morris Incorporated	PhilMorr
The Procter & Gamble Company	Proctr G
Pure Oil Co.	Pure Oil
Reading Company	Reading Co
Republic Steel Corporation	RepubStl
R. J. Reynolds Tobacco Company	Reyn Tob
Sears, Roebuck and Co.	Sears Ro
Shell Oil Company	Shell Oil
Skelly Oil Company	Skelly Oil
Southern California Edison Company	SouCalE
Southern Pacific Company	Sou Pac
Standard Oil Company	StOilNJ
Standard Oil Company of California	StOilCal
Sun Oil Company	Sun Oil
Swift Industries, Inc.	Swift Co
Texaco Inc.	Texaco
Tidewater Oil Co.	TidewatOil
Union Carbide Corporation	Un Carbide
Union Oil Company of California	UnOilCal

Company	*Abbreviation*
Union Pacific Railroad Company	UnPac
United Aircraft Corporation	UnitAirc
United States Steel Corporation	US Steel
United States Tobacco Company	USTobac
Vanadium Corp. of America	Vanadium
Westinghouse Electric Corporation	WestgEl
F. W. Woolworth Company	Woolworth
Xerox Corporation	XeroxCp

References

References are listed in alphabetical order. Where a study has appeared in more than one version (for example, as a dissertation and as a published article), only the most easily accessed has been referenced.

The resulting list provides a broad coverage of the topics covered in this book and offers a useful guide for further reading. For a more extensive bibliography on the subject, the reader is referred to Shannon P. Pratt, "Bibliography on Risks and Rates of Return for Common Stocks," *Financial Analysts Journal*, 24 (May–June 1968), 151–166.

1. Alexander, Sidney S. "Price Movements in Speculative Markets: Trends or Random Walks," *Industrial Management Review*, 2 (May 1961), 7–26. Reprinted in Cootner, *The Random Character of Stock Market Prices* [8].

2. ———. "Price Movements in Speculative Markets: Trends or Random Walks, Number 2," *Industrial Management Review,* 5 (Spring 1964), 25–46. Reprinted in Cootner, *The Random Character of Stock Market Prices* [8].

3. Arditti, Fred D. "Risk and the Required Return on Equity," *The Journal of Finance,* 22 (March 1967), 19–36.

4. Blume, Marshall E. "The Assessment of Portfolio Performance — An Application to Portfolio Theory." Unpublished Ph.D. dissertation, University of Chicago, 1968.

5. Brealey, Richard A. "The Character of Earnings Changes." Unpublished paper prepared for the Seminar on the Analysis of Security Prices, University of Chicago, May 1967.

6. ———. "Some Implications of the Comovement of Company Earnings." Unpublished paper prepared for the Seminar on the Analysis of Security Prices, University of Chicago, November 1968.

7. Brown, Philip, and Ball, Ray. "An Empirical Evaluation of Accounting Income Numbers," *Journal of Accounting Research.* 6 (Autumn 1968), 159–178.

8. Cootner, Paul H. (ed.) *The Random Character of Stock Market Prices.* Cambridge, Mass.: The MIT Press, 1964; paperback edition, 1967. This collection of articles includes *inter alia* those referenced 1, 2, 9, 21, 24, 27, 36, 43, 55.

9. Cootner, Paul H. "Stock Prices: Random Walks vs. Finite Markov Chains," *Industrial Management Review,* 3 (Spring 1962), 24–25. Reprinted under the title "Stock Prices: Random vs. Systematic Changes" in Cootner, *The Random Character of Stock Market Prices* [8].

10. Cragg, John G., and Malkiel, Burton F. "The Consensus and Accuracy of Some Predictions of the Growth of Corporate Earnings," *The Journal of Finance,* 23 (March 1968), 67–84.

11. ———. "Expectations and the Structure of Share Prices: An Empirical Study." Unpublished manuscript, 1967.

12. Crowell, Richard A. "Earnings Expectations, Security Valuation and the Cost of Equity Capital." Unpublished Ph.D. dissertation, Massachusetts Institute of Technology, 1967.

13. Douglas, George W. "Risk in the Equity Market: An Empirical Appraisal of Market Efficiency." Unpublished Ph.D. dissertation, Yale University, 1967.

14. Fama, Eugene F. "The Behavior of Stock Market Prices," *Journal of Business*, 38 (January 1965), 34–105.
15. ———. "Portfolio Analysis in a Stable Paretian Market," *Management Science*, 11 (January 1965), 404–419.
16. ———. "Risk, Return and Equilibrium." Report 6831, Center for Mathematical Studies in Business and Economics, University of Chicago, 1968.
17. ———. "Tomorrow on the New York Stock Exchange," *Journal of Business*, 38 (July 1965), 285–299.
18. Fama, Eugene F., and Blume, Marshall E. "Filter Rules and Stock Market Trading," *Journal of Business*, 39 (January 1966), 226–241.
19. Gaumnitz, Jack E. "Investment Diversification under Uncertainty: An Examination of the Number of Securities in a Diversified Portfolio." Unpublished Ph.D. dissertation, Stanford University, 1967.
20. Godfrey, Michael D., Granger, Clive W. J., and Morgenstern, Oskar. "The Random Walk Hypothesis of Stock Market Behavior," *Kyklos*, 17 (1964), 1–30.
21. Granger, Clive W. J., and Morgenstern, Oskar. "Spectral Analysis of New York Stock Market Prices," *Kyklos*, 16 (1963), 1–27. Reprinted in Cootner, *The Random Character of Stock Market Prices* [8].
22. Grayson, C. J. *Decisions Under Uncertainty: Drilling Decisions by Oil and Gas Operators*. Cambridge, Mass.: Harvard Business School, 1960. This book illustrates an application of utility theory.
23. Jensen, Michael C. "The Performance of Mutual Funds in the Period 1945–64." Unpublished paper presented at the Annual Meeting of the American Finance Association, December 1967.
24. Kendall, Maurice G. "The Analysis of Economic Time Series, Part I," *Journal of the Royal Statistical Society*, 96 (1953), 11–25. Reprinted in Cootner, *The Random Character of Stock Market Prices* [8].
25. King, Benjamin F. "Market and Industry Factors in Stock Price Behavior," *Journal of Business*, 39 (January 1966), 139–190.
26. Kisor, Manown, and Messner, Van A. "The Filter Approach and Earnings Forecasts—Part I." Unpublished manuscript, June 1968.

27. Larson, Arnold B. "Measurement of a Random Process in Futures Prices," *Food Research Institute Studies*, 1 (November 1960), 313–324. Reprinted in Cootner, *The Random Character of Stock Market Prices* [8].

28. Latane, Henry A., and Tuttle, Donald L. "An Analysis of Common Stock Price Ratios," *Southern Economic Journal*, 33 (January 1967), 343–354.

29. Lintner, John. "Security Prices, Risk and Maximal Gains from Diversification," *The Journal of Finance*, 20 (December 1965), 587–615.

30. ————. "The Valuation of Risk Assets and the Selection of Risky Investments in Stock Portfolios and Capital Budgets," *Review of Economics and Statistics*, 47 (February 1965), 13–37.

31. Lintner, John, and Glauber, Robert. "Higgledy Piggledy Growth in America." Unpublished paper prepared for the Seminar on the Analysis of Security Prices, University of Chicago, May 1967.

32. Little, Arthur D., Inc. "Studies of the Mutual Fund Industry." Report to the Investment Company Institute, June 1967.

33. Little, Ian M. D., and Rayner, A. C. *Higgledy Piggledy Growth Again*. Oxford: Basil Blackwell, 1966.

34. Mandelbrot, Benoit. "The Variation of Some Other Speculative Prices," *Journal of Business*, 40 (October 1967), 393–413.

35. Markowitz, Harry M. *Portfolio Selection: Efficient Diversification of Investments*. New York: John Wiley & Sons, Inc., 1959.

36. Moore, Arnold B. "Some Characteristics of Changes in Common Stock Prices," in Cootner, *The Random Character of Stock Market Prices* [8].

37. Moore, Geoffrey H., and Shiskin, Julius. *Indicators of Business Expansion and Contractions*. New York: National Bureau of Economic Research, 1967.

38. Murphy, Joseph. "Relative Growth of Earnings per Share — Past and Future," *Financial Analysts Journal*, 22 (Nov.–Dec. 1966), 73–76.

39. Ozga, S. A. *Expectations in Economic Theory*. London: Weidenfeld and Nicolson, 1965. This book provides a broad survey of modern utility theory.

40. Peters, William S. "The Psychology of Risk in Consumer Deci-

sions," in Fisk, George (ed.), *The Frontiers of Management Psychology*, New York: Harper and Row, 1964.

41. Pippenger, John. "The Behavior of Flexible Exchange Rates: Theory and Evidence." Unpublished Ph.D. dissertation, University of California at Los Angeles, 1966.

42. Pratt, Shannon P. "Relationship Between Risk and Rate of Return for Common Stocks." Unpublished D.B.A. dissertation, Indiana University, 1966.

43. Roberts, Harry V. "Stock Market 'Patterns' and Financial Analysis: Methodological Suggestions," *The Journal of Finance*, 14 (March 1959), 1–10. Reprinted in Cootner, *The Random Character of Stock Market Prices* [8].

44. Samuelson, Paul A. "General Proof That Diversification Pays" *Journal of Financial and Quantitative Analysis*, 2 (March 1967), 1–13.

45. ———. "Proof That Properly Anticipated Prices Fluctuate Randomly," *Industrial Management Review*, 6 (Spring 1965), 41–49.

46. Sharpe, William F. "Mutual Fund Performance," *Journal of Business*, 39 (January 1966), 119–138.

47. ———. "Risk-Aversion in the Stock Market: Some Empirical Evidence," *The Journal of Finance*, 20 (September 1965), 416–422.

48. Shiskin, Julius. "Systematic Aspects of Stock Price Fluctuations." Unpublished paper prepared for the Seminar on the Analysis of Security Prices, University of Chicago, May 1967.

49. Sprinkel, Beryl W. *Money and Stock Prices*. Homewood, Ill.: Richard D. Irwin, Inc., 1964.

50. Thorp, E. O., and Kassouf, S. *Beat the Market*. New York: Random House, Inc., 1967.

51. Tobin, James. "Liquidity Preference as Behavior Toward Risk," *Review of Economic Studies*, 25 (February 1958), 65–86.

52. Van Horne, James C., and Parker, George G. C. "The Random Walk Theory: An Empirical Test," *Financial Analysts Journal*, 23 (Nov.–Dec. 1967), 87–92.

53. ———. "Technical Trading Rules: A Comment," *Financial Analysts Journal*, 24 (July–Aug. 1968), 128–132.

54. Whitbeck, Volkert, and Kisor, Manown. "A New Tool in Investment Decision Making," *Financial Analysts Journal*, 19 (May–June 1963), 55–62.

55. Working, Holbrook. "Note on the Correlation of First Differences of Averages in a Random Chain," *Econometrica*, 28 (October 1960), 916–918. Reprinted in Cootner, *The Random Character of Stock Market Prices* [8].

56. ————. "Prices of Cash Wheat and Futures at Chicago since 1883," *Wheat Studies of the Stanford Food Institute*, II (1934), 75–124.

57. "How to Buy Stocks by the Calendar," *Fortune*, March 1965.

58. *NYSE Public Transaction Study*. New York: New York Stock Exchange, October 1966.

Index